"It's not
TOO LATE"

Dr. Timothy J. Schaub D.C.
Dr. Aaron Lewis Ph.D.

It's Not Too Late: Reclaiming Optimum Health No Matter How Young or Old You Are

ISBN 978-1-934466-54-4

Printed in the United States of America
First Printing

Foghorn Publishers
1 Congress Street, Suite 302
Hartford, CT 06114
860-904-6887
860-595-3788 fax
www.foghornpublishers.com
foghornpublisher@gmail.com

Foghorn Publishers is an imprint of Content Precision Inc.

Endorsements

From the beginning of chiropractic, chiropractors have always brought healing to children. The profession was built by the families who embraced this premise of life. We saw the children become adjusted, the life force returned within the body, and with time, discipline, along with a whole food diet, the children returned to full health, reaching their optimal potential.

Since 1962, The Children's Chiropractic Center Oklahaven has quietly served the most severely damaged children without federal, state or United Way funding, but only from the generosity of people who believe in a natural, drug-free way of life for our children.

Dr. Tim Schaub and his family have truly exemplified this way of life. With my love and admiration for this book, you will step into a journey of new life and health, happiness and wholeness.

Bobby Doscher, D.C. N.D.,
President/CEO The Children's Chiropractic Center
Oklahaven

"It's Not Too Late takes readers on a wonderful, but very significant journey into the world of drug-free solutions for healing. Dr. Lewis and Dr. Schaub have written this must-read practical guide that is full of vital information for those looking to regain and advance life's most cherished gift ... their health."

Dr. David Steinberg,
Past President, Connecticut Chiropractic Council and
Dr. Mehmet Oz's Board of Advisors, HealthCorps'

As a civil rights attorney, my life is fully vested in helping people to receive what belongs to them: equality, human rights, social freedoms, and protection against discrimination. Those rights often extend to the most vulnerable people within our society. I've traveled with both Dr. Schaub and Dr. Lewis to the Dominican Republic and witnessed firsthand how they both have given their lives to reach the poor, the hungry, and those most in need of healthcare.

I've seen Dr. Schaub adjust hundreds of people within a few short hours, just after listening to Dr. Lewis inspire people, young and old, to keep the faith. Both of these men live out loud, what this book says. You'll quickly learn that your health and wellness should not be optional. Read this book and choose life!

Tricia S. Lindsay Esq.
Mount. Vernon, New York

For the past few years, I've traveled to dozens of countries around the world helping to ensure that the principle and ethic of chiropractic will continue long after I'm gone. Dr. Schaub, chiropractor and Dr. Lewis, chiropractic ambassador have penned an important work that won't only keep chiropractic alive and well but even more, it'll keep you alive and well.

Dr. George B. Curry
President, International Chiropractic Association—
ICA's Chiropractor of the Year 2016, 2018

Acknowledgments

First and foremost, I want to acknowledge and express my never-ending gratitude to my life partner Dr. Dawn Stranges, Ph.D in Energy Medicine, the love of my life and the most exceptionally loving and caring woman I've ever known. Dawn Marguerite Stranges entered my life more than a decade ago, when I was at my very worst state of health. At that time, I was unable to walk without the support of a walker and confined to my bed or wheelchair. Dawn drove many hours on multiple occasions to make house calls for me to perform her remarkable healing energy work on me per the request of one of our mutual clients, Oscar.

Oscar was a double amputee who, quite frankly, didn't want me to die, so that I could continue to provide quality chiropractic care for him. As Dawn's and my professional relationship and mutual interest in clinical kinesiology, nutrition, health and healing grew, so did our love for each other, and for more than a decade now, we have become partners not only in practice but also in life. I never would have been able to take this journey without her.

Secondly, I want to thank my loyal and faithful practice members Mary Dick, Rose Roser, Jenn Potter and Missy Paczos who, during the time period of my life, when I had to close my offices in Syracuse and Cortland, NY, continued to care for me and made my personal well-being their priority. For that I am grateful.

My passionate and determined son, Tristan L. Schaub left his growing businesses in California, moved across the country to engage with me in our life work of improving chiropractic service throughout the globe. I am so proud of his work ethic, humor, diligence, and caring, that there are no words to express.

And finally, many profound thanks to my co-author, Dr. Aaron Lewis. His loving and wise guidance has led us on this journey of illuminating the magnificence of chiropractic for you, the reader. Thank you, Aaron.

The pages will not allow me to list every single person who has in one way or another impacted my life in a positive way. However, for the sake of time and page limitations I will list the names of several great people who have been a blessing to me over the years.

Dr. James Sigafoose
Dr. James W. Parker
Dr. Sid Williams
Dr. Anton Rittling
Dr. Dan White
Drs. Stephen Wechsler, Josh Pryer, and Rachel Murad
Dr. Bernard Straile
Dr. Larry Silverstein and Dr. Becky Keshmiri

Drs. Todd Stein
Dr. Ammitai Worob
Dr. Lynn Bayly
Dr. Linda Powers
Dr. Kevin Lalonde
Dr. Lance Loomis
Dr. Matt Antonelli
Drs. James Antun and Jayd M. Gray
Dr. Mitch Mally
Dr. Tony Posa
Dr. Jason Coburn
Dr. Darrel Asuncion
Dr. Adrienne Lara M.D.
Dr. Bill Stephan, M.D.
Dr. Matthew Bennett, M.D.
Dr. Channing Moon
Dr. Willie Kindred
Dr. Patricia McLean
Dr. Holly Schaub Lehman
Dr. Allen Knecht
Dr. Walter Holloway
Dr. Lloyd Steffensmeier
Dr. Deborah Macko
Dr. Blake Brown
Dr. Liam Miller
Dr. Andrea Paporto
Dr. David Pascal
Dr. Taylor Pascal
Dr. Gerald Coy
Dr. John D'Ambrosio
Dr. Roy Sweat

Dr. Bobby Doscher
Dr. Larry Wallace, O.D.
Barbara Korosec, RN, MS, ND
Patricia Serrao
Gregory Joseph
Kristen Augusta, LMT
Stephanie Fotes, LMT
Jeanne Kitt, LMT
Dr. Jennifer Royer
Dr. Tony Calamai
Drs. Bill Yoder and Mary Bakert Yoder
Dr. Brian Wofford
Dr. Jay Werder
Dr. Jamie Brenon-Lorich
Dr. Scott Banks
Heather Banks
Mericka Lehman
Jini Cerio
Cindy Trepasso
Mark Craig
Lance Kellogg
Mel Hanson
Kathie and Jim Delaney

Of course, I want to acknowledge Mary Ray Wood for her portrait photograph of me on our book cover. Thanks, Mary.

Disclaimer

The information contained in this book is the culmination of 40 years of experience in natural health care, working directly with thousands of patients of all ages. The statements made have not been evaluated by the FDA or the CDC. The opinions expressed are the opinions of the authors as well as other qualified natural health experts. The legal climate of our day requires me to tell you that you should not breathe, think, alter your medication, or start any exercise or diet program without first consulting a physician.

The author or the publisher of this material shall have neither liability nor responsibility to any person or entity with respect to any loss, damage, or injury caused or contained in this book. The information presented herein is not intended to be a substitute for medical counseling.

The information contained in this book is for informational purposes only and is not intended to diagnose, treat or cure disease or to take the place of care or treatment by a qualified, licensed health care professional. Your results will vary.

Respectfully,
Dr. Timothy Schaub

Dedication

This book is dedicated in memory of my visionary mother, **Dr. Ruth N. Schaub** and my gifted father, **Dr. William Schaub** and our dear friends **Dr. Cruse J. Howe** and **Dr. James Sigafoose**.

Table of Contents

Introduction...................................13

Chapter One
**The Fight of Your Life May Be
The Fight for Your Life**...................19

Chapter Two
In Drugs We Trust.......................33

Chapter Three
What Exactly Is Chiropractic?.......49

Chapter Four
If You Can't Read It, Don't Eat It.......63

Chapter Five
Back To Chiropractic...................79

Chapter Six
Life's A Mission..........................101

Chapter Seven
Take Back Your Life....................115

About The Author..........................128

Introduction

One of the strangest things I have come to discover is that while prescription drugs are now more widespread than any time in the history of the world, people are sicker than ever and still dying at a rapid rate. Both the pharmaceutical industry and the medical profession often use television commercials, billboard advertisements, and social media marketing to sway the masses into believing that if they will embrace a drug lifestyle that they will be better; that they will have good health. It doesn't take long to realize that this claim is simply not true. No matter how many drugs a person takes, drugs do not produce optimal health. Drugs never were intended to produce optimal health.

According to the Center for Disease Control in 2014 these were the leading causes of death:
Heart disease: 614,348
Cancer: 591,699
Chronic lower respiratory diseases: 147,101

Accidents (unintentional injuries): 136,053
Stroke (cerebrovascular diseases): 133,103
Alzheimer's disease: 93,541
Diabetes: 76,488
Influenza and pneumonia: 55,227

Except for accidents, there are several prescription drugs for each of these sicknesses on the market, yet not one of them cures the problem. Heart disease, cancer, and respiratory diseases still make up nearly 1.4 million deaths each year. Yet, people still live by the motto "In Drugs We Trust." Are people intrinsically brainwashed to believe that something that never cures them is worth continuing? This is not to say that there aren't medications that are life sustaining and that some people need in order to survive. We all realize that there are medical breakthroughs and research that have helped people. What I disagree with most is the culture that has trained people to believe that drugs equal good health, despite that evidence proves otherwise.

> No matter how many drugs a person takes, drugs do not produce optimal health.

The New York Times Bestseller *Rich Dad Poor Dad* which sold more than 26 million copies detailed the life of author Robert Kiyosaki growing up in Hawaii. It discusses about how his "rich dad," the father of his childhood best friend and his "poor dad," his biological father had totally different thoughts about money and how to obtain financial freedom. Both fathers taught the author how to achieve success in life, from disparate perspectives. His biological father who had a Ph.D. struggled to make ends meet as his choices reflected the majority of how most people lived out their financial lives in society, landing them into poverty.

The rich dad, had no college training at all but rather had financial sensibility that catapulted him from mediocrity to super rich by becoming financially literate. It became evident to Kiyosaki which father's approach made more financial sense and that was the one that he pursued. In the same thought pattern, I often feel as if I were raised with two sets of parents, also; good parents and bad parents. My good parents would be my biological parents, Drs. William and Ruth Schaub, who were both exceptional chiropractors. As children, neither I nor my brother or sisters were immunized. When I say that, what I should say is that we were never vaccinated because vaccination does not necessarily equate to immunization. Even as an adult I have never been vaccinated. I've never been given an antibiotic, or even an aspirin, or over the counter medications.

However, the topic of vaccination and immunization I will deal with later in the book. As a child, my oldest sister Heather, who is married to a chiropractor, Dr. Scott Banks, and my older sister, Dr. Holly Schaub Lehman, who is also a chiropractor, were not fed the typical American diet. Back then, kids grew up eating Wonder Bread and drinking sodas. That was their normal diet. My siblings and I were given non-genetically modified soy bread that fortunately, during those years, only cost about 30 to 35 cents per loaf. The bread we ate was baked by a local baker around the corner from our house. Joe Stupke's soy bread not only tasted great but was also truly nourishing. We weren't served soda in our home. We drank water, water my father fortified with fresh grown wheatgrass that he grew in numerous shoeboxes around our kitchen to alkalize the water.

I can clearly remember a time when I was 6 years old. I was climbing a chain link fence at the local elementary school baseball diamond, while my dad and I were watching my older brother play ball. As I got to the top of the fence, my right arm draped over the sharp protruding wires. Suddenly, I lost my grip and simultaneously ripped my arm open from just above my wrist to right below my elbow. This accident left me with a deep bloody gash.

My dad swiftly stuffed my arm with paper towels that he had in his pocket, applied a tourniquet and picked me up and carried me home. When we got home, he immediately bandaged the cut, dressing my wound with his seemingly magical mineral ointment called Brabon, which was manufactured by an organic chemist, Dr. HC Weber, from Telford, Pennsylvania.

Then he gave me a chiropractic adjustment to my cervical spine to maximize the neuro-vascular circulation into my shoulder and arm and I immediately felt my wound healing. I was fine. I was healing—naturally. Other parents would have handled the same situation differently by first calling an ambulance, going to the emergency room to get treated with antibiotics, pain killing drugs, and multiple stitches. My dad's method not only did the job, but I have perfect function in my right arm until this day, without the use of drugs or surgery - and with hardly any scarring!

My bad parents, are not actually biological at all. However, I was born into a society that gave them to me from birth. These are the parents of industry and profit. These are the parents that continue to do things that are totally counterproductive to your health and overall well-being. These parents teach that every time you feel sick, medicate yourself. These parents teach, if you have back pain, a sciatica or bulging disc, get surgery. If you have a headache, don't relax; use Advil or Motrin. I chose not to listen to the other set of parents. While I was fortunate to have another set of parents teaching me from childhood, I quickly realized that the clear majority of people in the country relied heavily on the status quo, which pushed drugs for more profit rather than health and total wellness.

Being a second-generation chiropractor, I went into this profession with the clear intent of getting people well. My sister did also. It didn't take me long to realize that people getting and staying sick was the Western political pharmacological underlying objective of the Big Pharma, or the Western political medical industry. Being well doesn't

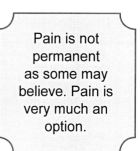

Pain is not permanent as some may believe. Pain is very much an option.

pay the bills for the medical practitioners. So, it would be in their vested interest to make sure that you stay sick for as long as you live. I asked my friend Dr. Aaron Lewis, who is not a chiropractor but a professional writer of more than 160 books and a lifelong advocate of chiropractic care to join with me in writing this book with one simple message to the reader: It's Not Too Late.

> You have options, and that is what this book is all about.

Whether you are in your eighties and have experienced poor health for decades or if you are in your teens and you've been injured badly playing sports or cheerleading, you can still achieve optimal health. Pain is not permanent as some may believe. Pain is very much an option. You have options and that is what this book is all about. I will share stories about people and even animals that received a second chance at total wellness in life. You'll travel on a journey of my life and the lives of many others to prove to you what I've already mentioned, that it's not too late to get your health back and begin to live the life that you deserve.

Dr. Timothy J. Schaub—

Homer, New York

Chapter One

THE FIGHT OF YOUR LIFE MAY BE THE FIGHT FOR YOUR LIFE

The strangest thing is that my entire life I've been fighting. In fact, I come from a lineage of fighters. When my mother, Dr. Ruth Schaub, was pregnant with me at the seasoned age of 47 years young, she encountered an awful fall down a flight of stairs. She was hurt very badly. Her entire lower back was severely injured. My father even took x-rays of her to access the damage to her body. Although she had been badly hurt, the x-ray clearly showed me as an embryo in her lower abdomen area. Despite the fall, I was fine and intact. Today, I still have those x-rays. My point is that even in my mother's womb, before I officially began my journey on earth, I was fighting for my life.

My mother having encountered the accident as well, could have easily died from such a horrific fall, but she fought forward to recover and deliver me into the world. Fighting was somewhat normal for both me and my family. It was that spirit of perseverance that commanded my footsteps and brought me to the place I am today.

My mother was cut from a different strap. I mean, during a time where not many women went to college at all, but rather pursued homemaking paths, my mother graduated from Cornell University in 1934 with a degree in pre-med and economics.

My Parent's Training

Graduating from Cornell in and of itself was a fight forward for women's rights for higher education. After Cornell, my mother decided to become a chiropractor. Although she had the training to become a medical doctor, she realized early on that a natural health path was what she believed in and would stand for. It was at the Eastern Chiropractic Institute in New York City where she met my father Dr. William Schaub. Interestingly, it was called Eastern because it was the eastern branch of the acclaimed Palmer College, headquartered in Davenport, Iowa, founded by Daniel David Palmer, the father of chiropractic.

> When your immune system is attacked, the very thing that is supposed to keep you well no longer has the capacity to do so, leaving you vulnerable to multiple attacks...

During my parents' first day at the Eastern Chiropractic Institute of New York, they were sitting in a classroom in the semi-round and my mom and dad were sitting next to each other. My mom and dad had just met that day for the first time, so they knew very little about each other's character. However, my father would quickly come to realize that my mother was nonconformist, as was the mindset of many chiropractors during that time. My mother was an out-of-the-box thinker and seemed to welcome challenges, especially those that supported what she dearly believed. My mother was willing to fight for her convictions.

During their first class, which was a Neurophysiology class that was taught by a practicing chiropractor from New York City, the United States Federal Marshals abruptly entered the classroom during his lecture, and handcuffed, shackled and arrested the instructor, claiming that he was practicing medicine without a license. In fact, he wasn't practicing medicine at all. But from the early days of chiropractic there was persecution and aggression against the profession because of what it represented; healthcare without drugs or surgery. That concept was very much misunderstood. Later my parents learned that this was a staged attempt designed to scare at least some of the new students from pursuing a career in chiropractic.

To some degree, it worked, because when the professor was dragged out of class, after having been arrested in front of all his students, nearly all the women in the class got up and left, and never came back. About half of the men in the class similarly left and never returned. My dad's interest in my mother become even more keen as he realized that she didn't scare easily. She was tough as nails and they often considered her the first liberated woman, with my dad's permission. During class, my mother leaned over and said to my dad, "Bill, we must really be onto something here; if they're that scared of letting us learn about chiropractic then we'd better stick around and see what's up."

My mother, Dr. Ruth Norgren first practiced on Decatur Avenue in the Bronx and then moved to Mount Vernon, New York where she was formally mentored by one very well-known chiropractor, Dr. Lyndon Lee, who I was blessed to get to know as a teenager. He was an impressive fully white-haired older gentleman with an athletic build. He had the most perfect posture of anyone I've ever had the opportunity to meet. Just as a professional boxer or an Olympian athlete must be trained in their sport to be the best, great chiropractors also must be well trained.

Often, that training may require being exposed to uncomfortable circumstances and fighting through it. That was their story, their fight, and their victory of which I was born into—a real legacy. My father took care of more than 350 multigenerational families that he wouldn't refer to as patients, but rather as his "people." Both of my parents adjusted animals; dogs and horses as well, and left a lasting mark on the people of the entire New York southern tier region. It's been said that everyone has a story; here is mine.

Along Came a Spider

I have always deeply admired people who served in the military. I've admired not only their commitment to serving and protecting our country but also the courage that they exercise in battle. In battle, there is always the possibility that you may not return home. Many of our military men and women make a conscious decision to fight, realizing that serving the greater good is always a priority. That is commendable. Personally, I have never served in battle; neither have I ever killed anyone. I've never seen bloody, dying bodies presented at my feet for care in a hospital.

In fact, I had never experienced a major sickness of any kind. As a boy, I had a severely cut arm. And once I had a serious strep throat. But that was all. I had lived for nearly four and a half decades and had been in nearly perfect health. My health was far better than most people who were 44 years old. Back then, I worked

> It's so important to ensure that the spine is always in proper alignment so that the rest of the body will function properly.

consistently at being HEALTHY, mentally, physically, emotionally, and spiritually. With each decade of my life I was getting healthier, fitter, stronger and physiologically younger. Age didn't bother me one bit as increasing age became my benchmark for increasingly better health.

It was my plan to meet all my life goals, to take exceptional care of my family, and to live to the ripe old age of 120.

Retirement wasn't in my consciousness. I was working in the profession that I loved and wanted to do it until I made my transition. I often jested that I wanted the epitaph of my tombstone to read, "Here Lies Dr. Tim Schaub – ALL USED UP." But on April fool's day everything changed. And my fight began, the fight for my life.

A fierce hunter called a "Brown Recluse Spider" bit me. The bite was painful. But I didn't think much of that as in most insect bites are painful on some level. I didn't overthink it. I just thought that I was bit and that I'd use an antiseptic and it'd go away in a short while. Boy, was I wrong. That bite began the path to a long and painful journey toward declining health, nearly leading to my death. Later, I learned that these female spiders do not eat for several months except for eating the males that impregnate them. They do not take the time to spin webs to catch little insects or flies. Rather, they are reclusive; hiding out, looking for prey; stalking their «prime rib» of meat.

That is what this little bitch did to me. While I was in bed under my comfy covers, she quietly and rather stealthily injected me with her digestive enzymes to anesthetize my nerves, and tenderize the meat on the front of my right knee as I was dosing off to sleep early that evening around 7:30 P.M. I went to bed early that night because I had an early day the next day, planning to awake at 4:21 A.M. My day as usual was meticulously organized and planned out. Awakening at 4:21 A.M. would give me just the right amount of time to take care of my two sibling Saint Bernards; Sister Sissy and her Big Brother Julius.

After that I would eat a healthy breakfast; drive 40 miles to get to the gym; workout hard for an hour; shower and get to my office by 7:00 A.M. to adjust 35 or so patients in my chiropractic center before noontime. Little did I know that after this reclusive assailant had injected me with her digestive enzymes, she had sucked out 1-2 square inches of my meat. She then injected me with a potentially fatal poisonous neurotoxin. Not only was my battlefield being prepared, but my hopes for continuing with optimum health and vitality were being diminished. This was a war, a war for my survival.

Attack Against my Immune System

Never in a million years had I ever thought that a little ole spider could do such crippling damage to the human body. Maybe they could cause a rash or a little discomfort, but not only anymore than that. This spider was not the world's most deadly spider but she was certainly a part of the "special forces" of arachnids. The Brown Recluse Spiders are the only carnivorous spiders on the planet. If a Brown Recluse is successful at anesthetizing her prey, and she takes the time to completely inject her poison into her subject, the prey's immune system will often become fully compromised.

Researchers have found that nearly 44% of these spider's victims die soon after their system has been inoculated

> It's so important to ensure that the spine is always in proper alignment so that the rest of the body will function properly.

with this poison. Miss Recluse had injected a fatal dose of venom inside of me. She may have also infused some parasites after eating nearly two square inches of flesh from my knee. Think about if a human didn't eat anything for 9 months and when they finally did eat they'd have to consume a 1,000-pound steer all raw. That's the best way that I can describe the magnitude of this spider's undertaking. This was just the beginning of my troubles.

After being bitten by this spider, the average person would have swelled up within 12-48 hours. I was significantly healthier than the average person, so my system fought against the swelling by trying to resist its effects on me. My swelling didn't begin until the 11th day. Although I was unusually tired, I attributed that to having to meet exorbitant child and alimony payments that the court had ordered a year earlier following a beleaguered divorce. So, I didn't overthink it much. I did not connect it with the bite.

Even though I was a strapping 6 foot 3 inches tall with a solid muscle build, I felt more like a helpless infant unable to defend himself against this battle. During Roman times the term infantry came about as they would put the youngest and smallest children in the front line of the battle; the infants to go first before the skilled warrior came. They were the sacrifices. I began to relate to this idea of self-sacrifice as my health began to spiral downward quickly.

My goals swiftly changed from living life to the optimum to merely surviving. I was dying and doing anything that I could to just stay alive. It's one thing to attack my flesh. That can be cleaned, treated, and on its way to healing. But when your immune system is attacked, the very thing that is supposed to keep you well no longer has the capacity to do so, leaving you vulnerable to multiple attacks in places you wouldn't dream of.

Attacked from Many Sides and Losing Ground

I was losing ground in this battle as one thing led to another. This one bite began the path to one sickness after another. It didn't seem real what was happening to me. Three months after the bite in July, I developed a pilonidal cyst, which looked very similar to the original bite. It formed at the bottom of my tailbone. So that it wouldn't get larger or infected, I surgically removed it. During this same time, I began to lose all function of balance and coordination. It became increasingly difficult for me to stay focused. It was even hard for me to read books, articles, or even short sentences.

My proprioception, which is the sense of the relative position of neighboring parts of the body and strength of effort being employed in movement was also affected.

If I were sitting on a grade level flat surface in a parked car I would feel like the car was sliding backward. It was scary. Driving or riding over bridges created an unusually terrifying experience for me. Sometimes, I would look at a sign or billboard, and think it would say one thing with a picture on it – then I would look back, for a second view, and realize it was entirely a different picture and sign. My vision and perception was changing.

Since I knew that the brain is the central part of my central nervous system, these dyslexic-type symptoms while extremely annoying to me didn't come as a surprise to me. If brain function is off kilter, then the entire body will follow suit. That's why it's so important to ensure that the spine is always in proper alignment so that the rest of the body will function properly. That following September, three months after the pilonidal cyst formed I thought, a second bite appeared on my left leg. In actuality, it wasn't a second bite at all but rather it was actually the exit hole for the venom. It left a shiny black necrotic hole and permanent scarring on the inside of my leg.

The infectious venom had spread up my right leg, through my pelvis and lower back and was attempting to exit through my left lower leg. The neurotoxins poisoned my peroneal nerve and caused crippling in my left big toe and paralysis of my toes so that I have no toe spread in either leg, even until today. This immobility of my feet and damage to the leg muscles has resulted in multiple ulcer formations in different areas of my feet and toes.

This infection caused some kidney damage and damage to the muscles in my left legs and feet, and caused disturbances to the lymphatic system in my leg and foot.

It caused swelling, periodic cellulitis and mild lymphedema, all of which have been helped through chiropractic care, energy medicine, manual lymph drainage, colloidal silver and other natural topical agents such as tea tree and lavender oils. The venom of the Brown Recluse Spider is also a hemotoxin, which means it causes injuries to the blood; a type of poisoning which makes the red blood cells burst so that the kidneys can no longer adequately process the damaged blood. This hemotoxin has since been found to cause massive MRSA - like infection, which isn't easily treatable since it is resistant to commonly used antibiotics.

Pressing Forward

These years were the most difficult years of my life. Despite how difficult it was, I made the decision that I wanted to live, I had to live, and that it was not too late to recover my health. As the years passed along, I had to painfully deal with the struggle of walking with crippled feet and ulcers. I lost a great deal of muscle mass and my spine became subluxated and fixated in my dorsal-lumbar junction, (which means that at the junction between my mid-back and my lower back) my spine shifted out of alignment and locked up. This caused me to have a very antalgic crooked posture, bending forward and to the side.

These subluxations also caused a significant amount of back pain. The condition also caused my feet and legs to become freezing cold. Soon I experienced marked atrophy in the muscles of my hands as well as nerve paresthesia shooting pains in the 3rd, 4th and 5th fingers of both of my hands. Periodontal disease also occurred when my dentists found 6mm pockets around my loose teeth. For a number of years, I would visit his office for cleaning every 3 months but they would have to inject large amounts of Novocain into my gums and could only clean ¼ of my teeth at a session.

Eventually, I developed an intolerance to the Novocain and would find myself feeling the effects of the injections hours after my cleaning was over, as I was driving home from their office I would feel drunk. I was unable to sleep, only sleeping 1 ½ to 3 hours each night for nearly three years. It was also a specific type of chiropractic care that helped me to overcome both the insomnia and the allergic reaction to the Novocain. Chiropractic care also helped me reduce food allergies that resulted from the bite.

As I recovered, I required the use of two canes because I could not stand up without the use of them. Sadly, I was forced into closing both of my chiropractic offices. I couldn't drive because my response time in my legs was too poor to brake quickly if necessary, I needed a wheelchair, motorized cars, and walkers just to become mobilized.

> You must have a mindset to fight forward, realizing that maintaining your life may be the fight of your life

My first flight after the sickness was to stay with my sister Holly Schaub Lehman, who is also a Chiropractor in Albuquerque, NM, where she saw to it that I was adjusted regularly and assisted me in my daily activities of life in general. For this I will be eternally in her debt and forever grateful for her kindness.

After about a month there, not bending over patients and not having the stress of appointments and practice I returned home and attempted to see a few loyal patients out of my home office. I was determined to live life again. I felt that the worst was behind me and I had the resolve to live, to press forward and to begin living out my passion of helping thousands of people to receive their healing. It hasn't been easy at all, but it has been the most significant lesson learned up until this point in my life. Realistically, I should be dead and buried. I'm here. I'm alive. I have another chance.

If I could live through such tragic circumstances I believe that you, your loved ones and friends can fight through some tough challenges also. First you must have a mindset to fight forward, realizing that maintaining your life may be the fight of your life—one that's well worth it.

Chapter Two

IN DRUGS WE TRUST

The drug industry is possibly the most profitable and fastest growing industry in the world. It's more profitable than the cattle, poultry and seafood industries combined. Why is that? It's sad yet simple. The drug industry uses strategic marketing and advertising campaigns to convince consumers to buy their products. Drug companies spend billions of dollars on advertising and marketing annually reaping larger-than-life profits from their adverting investments. Plainly put, they aim at convincing people to trust in drugs. They do this through the power of repetition and auto suggestion. The more you hear something the greater your chances are of believing it, even if it's a lie. That's the power of programming.

Much of their strategy consists of scare tactics. People are moved by

> Iatrogenic deaths are the leading cause of death in the United States

fear. Let's face it, most people want to live, and will do anything within their power to live a little longer. People who are dealing with sicknesses, especially those that can lead to sudden death, will take whatever advice their doctors or drug companies give them to preserve their life. That isn't necessarily a bad thing to take advice from skilled professionals. What's bad is when the advice that is being given isn't proven and tested. Or worse yet, is when the drug being offered has the potential to do more harm than good.

Earlier I mentioned the leading causes of death according to the Center for Disease Control. The real leading cause of death that does not show on their list, as it does not manifest as a physical sickness of the body, is iatrogenic deaths. Iatrogenesis is known as the "inadvertent and preventable induction of disease or complications by the medical treatment or procedures of a physician or surgeon." Researchers have found that America's leading cause of death is not heart disease or cancer: it's conventional medicine. Studies have shown that that the iatrogenic death rate in the United States alone (death caused by doctors and/or medical treatments) is 783,936 annually.

That number represents 84,059 more deaths than those caused by heart disease in 2001 and 230,865 more deaths than those caused by cancer. In a ten-year period, scientists have predicted that iatrogenic deaths will total about 7.8 million. That is more than all the casualties combined from all United States wars in its entire history. While these high death tolls are unbelievable, most people do not even realize how high of a risk factor taking prescription drugs is. While the facts concerning the high death rate associated with prescription drug use are readily available, it is often disguised using words such as "iatrogenic," "induced," "evoked," and "elicited."

These words are used to indemnify doctors from lawsuits related to malpractice. So, one way to free doctors from liability is to use fancy buzzwords that most people won't readily recognize. If you don't know what a word means then you probably won't have a strong guard against it or its effects. The second way to free doctors is to brainwash the public into believing that the drugs are harmless. Or a better way of stating it, is that the drugs can bring about more potential good than it can harm. They do this through constant and repeated commercial advertising. They will advertise until you become a believer and a user.

> Iatrogenesis – Inadvertent and preventable induction of disease or complication by physicians and surgeons

Since Boots Pharmaceuticals aired its first commercial on May 19, 1983 of a pain reliever called Rufen, a competitor to the popular Motrin, the drug industry has recognized the power of marketing directly to the consumer as being vastly more profitable than marketing their drugs to medical doctors as they previously had done for a century prior. It would seem ethical to market prescription drugs to medical doctors rather than his or her patients, particularly since the average person does not know how the drugs properly work in their bodies, if the drug has lethal side effects, or if the drug has the propensity to trigger adverse reactions in normally functioning parts of the body.

However, the profits are higher and more impulsive when you market to the end user directly. Generally, people believe whatever they continually hear. They buy into the perceived benefits, especially when it comes through the television and internet commercials. And when people are sick and in need of healing, they'll take temporary benefits in exchange for the loss of something else. Print ads work effectively as well. Just two years prior to the Rufen advertisement, the world's oldest drug and chemical company, Merck released an ad in 1981 promoting their pneumonia vaccine.

More than 35 years later, millions of people willingly get vaccinated for pneumonia and flu each year, falsely believing that the vaccine guards them from sicknesses. More than 42 million people each year get the flu shot. Interestingly, a large amount of people who receive the flu shots each year get the flu. It's often offered free of charge at local pharmacies. After all these years, one thing is for sure, the marketing worked. Unfortunately, ethics rarely plays a role when the trade off is big profits. The late Senator Ted Kennedy from Massachusetts said, "These ads almost certainly encourage the unnecessary use of these drugs."

The "unnecessary use" of drugs is exactly what the big pharmaceuticals want. What most people fail to realize is that your health and wholeness is not the objective of the drug companies, profit is. While drugs may sustain you or even help some people in life threatening circumstances, drugs don't make you well. They were never intended to. They're intended to make big profits. If they continue to make big profits, then death casualties really do not matter. To the Big Pharma, death is just the high cost for doing business.

How Much Profit Is Enough?

In the world, there are more than 23,000 pharmaceutical and bio-tech companies, 572 of which are publicly traded. Let's consider the ten largest pharmaceutical companies account for $440 billion dollars in annual sales and employ more than 868,000 people. That's only the top ten companies. If I were to add the revenues from the entire list of drugs companies, the industry collectively would rake in revenues and profits in the trillions of dollars. The truth is that when their earning capacity becomes that strong, there is very little that can be done to regulate unscrupulous practices, as they have plenty of money to pay their fines and continue in business.

> Millions of people willingly get vaccinated for pneumonia each year, falsely believing that the vaccine guards them from sicknesses.

The anti-inflammatory drug Vioxx, which Merck released back in 1999, was promoted in a 60-second spot that featured Olympian figure skater Dorothy Hamill explaining how the drug had helped her overcome her osteoarthritis. Five years after, Merck recalled the drug because of concerns about increased risk of heart attack or stroke. Despite the risk involved with the drug, Vioxx was already bringing in $2.5 billion in annual sales. Profits that high make heart attack and stroke a secondary issue. And unfortunately, many people are conditioned to accept the continued use of harmful drugs as normal, as long as the FDA approves it.

So began an article by Andrew Ross Sorkin in the New York Times. Actually, Sorkin's title was taken from Harvard professor, Bill George, who asked: "Is the role of leading large pharmaceutical companies to discover lifesaving drugs or to make money for shareholders through financial engineering?" Professor George's question was prompted by the spate of companies seeking to merge with foreign companies (in this case, Pfizer trying to acquire AstraZeneca) with the ultimate intent of lowering their corporate tax rates. However, these comments play on the public's concern that the pharmaceutical industry is primarily focused on making money – not drugs." (John LaMattina, Forbes Magazine JUL 29, 2014 @ 09:03 AM)

Based on research, drug companies focus on profits. They create drugs that offer minimum improvements over existing therapies, yet charge unconscionable prices for them. Successfully running a biopharmaceutical company is an expensive and high risk endeavor. So, if you cannot generate an enormous profit, you won't be able to stay in business. This model makes it difficult for these companies to place a value on research that can provide cost effective ways for people to get medicine that produces favorable and long term results. That is a recipe for failure. The way they make money is to continue to produce drugs of little or no effect that the consumer continues to use despite experiencing little if any positive change.

Business people realize the fundamentals of doing business. A business owes its loyalty to its shareholders. Its responsibility is to produce a profit for those who've bought stock into the company. The purpose of the corporation is not to provide the consumer of its products with products that work or promote healthy results. If the company makes money for its shareholders and you die in the process, they've done their job successfully. It's not about keeping you alive. It's about making profits— huge profits.

Biblical Origin of Pharma

Why are so many people deceived into leading a drug lifestyle? With the long list of possible fatal side effects that are clearly disclosed on television commercials and written clearly on labels, why do so many people still choose to use and abuse prescription drugs? Maybe the Bible could give us a clue. The English word for "pharmacy" comes from the Greek word "pharmakeia". It means "sorcery" and "witchcraft". The word "druggist" or "pharmacist" comes from the Greek word "pharmakon" meaning "poisoner." When people use drugs they are literally influenced by another spirit, a spirit of sorcery.

Something else is controlling their mind, actions, and thoughts.

> A business' responsibility is to produce a profit for those who've bought stock into the company.

What the druggists give is poison. Again, this is not to say that there is no drug that has been or will ever be useful. We know all too well that there is a list of life saving medications that when used under the right circumstances and conditions have literally saved millions of lives. There are medications that have done good for humankind. What we are opposed to is a system that has controlled the minds of the masses into believing that every health problem can be solved with the use of a particular drug. That's a lie!

What you need to realize is that to regain your life and begin to live life to the optimum, you must recognize what you are up against. One of the main things that is stealing life from their masses is the dependency on drugs, or shall I say, the drug addictions of the masses. People are really addicted to drugs. So, when we use the word sorcery and witchcraft we do so to impress upon you how controlling, seductive or deceiving an entire for-profit industry is. It's pure deception. However, so many people have bought into that deception because "everybody seems to be doing it." Everybody is getting the flu shot. Everybody's kids are getting vaccinated, despite the connections to autism and neurologically related diseases.

… for by thy sorceries (pharmakeia) were all nations deceived. Revelations 18:23

Ask Your Doctor?

Our society has become romanticized by the idea of medical doctors to the point that their advice is often unquestioned by the masses. We are often given the warning, before using this or that product consult your doctor. Before exercising consult your doctor. Before getting checked by a chiropractor, consult your doctor. The list goes on and on. This dependency on the doctor has become pandemic. More than that, it's a constant repetition that has a hypnotizing and brainwashing effect. It makes people who are fully capable of making intelligent decisions for themselves unhealthily reliant on the doctor's advice.

Very few people question, "What if the doctor is wrong? What if my doctor does not understand my condition? What if my doctor isn't trained to understand what I am experiencing health wise? Should I still seek his or her advice? What if the drugs that were recommended are experimental and they've not been thoroughly tested for safety, should I still use them? What if the drugs that

I've been given produce an adverse effect or cause illness to spring up in another part of my body, should I simply trust the advice given?"

> A business' responsibility is to produce a profit for those who've bought stock into the company.

Dr. Lewis has a beautiful granddaughter named Ava, who at the time of this writing is about 22 months young. When she was born, her mother, Amber took her to the doctor for her regular checkup when she was just nearing 2 months. The doctor recommended 6 vaccines for her. They recommended a second dose of 5 more vaccines just two months later, and then 7 more two months after that. At one year's young, they recommended six more vaccines to be given all of which are "recommended by the state." Dr. Lewis raised his daughter on holistic foods and on getting regularly adjusted by the chiropractor. So, his children were not over vaccinated as most children are.

Amber decided to ask the doctor why were certain vaccines needed and why they were mandatory. The strangest thing happened. The doctor didn't know. She could not answer her questions about the vaccines that her office swore by. What Amber realized was that many of the vaccines that are being given to children have no real strong purpose at all but are rather a part of protocol for the doctors and, of course, the drug manufacturers.

How could it be that drugs are given in mass doses to babies, yet the doctors cannot firmly argue why they are needed?

She asked the doctor and didn't get an answer, because the doctor didn't know. What the pediatrician did know is that they were taught to follow protocol, follow systems, follow what you were trained to do, even if it doesn't make relevant sense. Fortunately, Amber refused the majority of the vaccines as she didn't want her infant to be affected by the poison in those vaccinations. Good for her!

Some doctors are a bit savvier than others and may answer your question. But that doesn't mean that the answer is correct. The answer that they give most frequently is just a coined answer that has become accepted as true though their research that proves otherwise. This is what they'll claim each vaccine does for your child. But they never tell you the whole truth about the dangerous complications which research by independent medical sources have determined to have caused multiple disorders and dysfunction and damage to the nervous system.

HepB protects against hepatitis B (infection of the liver). HepB is given in three shots. The first shot is given at the time of birth. Most states require HepB vaccination for a child to enter school. Yet denying your children education goes against your rights and you can be excluded from this provision based on religious rights and/or personal convictions concerning health and anti-vaccinations.

RV supposedly protects against rotavirus, a major cause of diarrhea. RV is given in two or three doses, depending on the vaccine used. Diarrhea is simply loose and watery stools. It isn't serious and usually corrects itself without any medication.

DTaP protects against diphtheria, tetanus, and pertussis (whooping cough). It requires five doses during infancy and childhood. DTaP boosters are then given during adolescence and adulthood.

Hib protects against Haemophilus influenzae type b. This infection was the leading cause of bacterial meningitis. Hib vaccination is given in four doses.

PCV protects against pneumococcal disease. PCV is given in a series of four doses.

IPV protects against polio and is given in four doses. In 2016 only 42 people were affected in the world. In 2014, the disease only spread throughout Afghanistan, Nigeria and Pakistan.

Influenza (flu) protects against the flu. This is a seasonal vaccine that is given yearly. Flu shots can be given to your child each year, starting at age 6 months. The Flu season can run from September through May. Neither myself nor Dr. Lewis has ever had a flu shot.

MMR protects against measles, mumps, and rubella (German measles). MMR is given in two doses. The first dose is recommended for infants between 12 and 15 months. The second dose is usually given between ages 4 and 6 years. However, it can be given as soon as 28 days after the first dose.

Varicella protects against chickenpox. Varicella is recommended for all healthy children. It's given in two doses. This is the same virus that once in your system become the basis for shingles later in life. However, they don't disclose that information to mothers with young children.

HepA protects against hepatitis A.

Do they tell you what vaccines have been connected to?

Anaphylactic shock
Aseptic meningitis, meningitis
Bell's palsy, facial palsy, isolated cranial nerve palsy
Blood disorders such as thrombocytopenic purpura (a disease that destroys platelets need for clotting)
Brachial neuritis
Cerebrovascular accident (stroke)
Chronic rheumatoid arthritis
Convulsions, seizures, febrile seizure
Death
Encephalopathy and encephalitis (brain swelling)
Hearing loss
Guillain-Barré syndrome
Immune system disorders
Lymphatic system disorders
Multiple sclerosis
Myocarditis
Nervous system disorders
Neurological syndromes including autism

Paralysis and myelitis including transverse myelitis
Peripheral neuropathy
Pneumonia and lower respiratory infections
Skin and tissue disorders including eczema
Sudden infant death syndrome (SIDS)
Tinnitus (ringing in the ears)
Vaccine-strain versions of chicken pox, measles, mumps, polio, influenza, meningitis, yellow fever, and pertussis
Vasculitis (inflammation of blood vessels)

The United States Food and Drug Administration (USDA), does not require safety assessments for vaccines nor do they require toxicity studies before they are distributed, since vaccines have not been viewed as inherently toxic. The use of fancy language to camouflage the truth. Instead of calling vaccines toxic, which they are, they legally define vaccines as unavoidably unsafe. Many vaccines that pose a great risk to your overall health are given to children. However, children are not the only targets of vaccines. Adults are offered influenza vaccines, vaccines for sexually transmitted diseases, and vaccines for pregnant women despite the fact that the package inserts say that the product has not been tested on pregnant women.

Over time, vaccines have gotten out of control. Being vaccinated has become the unfortunate norm. During the 1960s very few children were vaccinated. The Center for Disease Control recommends that children have more than 30 vaccines by the time they reach 6 years of age. They are recommending nearly 30 more between the ages of 6 and 18. Despite all the vaccines being given in the United States alone, children are not healthy, but sicker than ever.

> More than 50% of children suffer from a chronic illness. (According to Academic Pediatrics)
> One in six children in the United States has a learning disability (CDC)
> Cancer has become the leading cause of death by disease in our children (NIH/National Cancer Institute)
> Autism rates have soared from 1 in 10,000 in 1990 to 1 in 68 today (CDC)

So, when you are encouraged to ask your doctor, you may want to consider that his or her answer will always be biased, unless your medical doctor is open to naturopathic and chiropractic care. If they are fully medically minded, then they will be at a major disadvantage with regards to answering health questions without considering toxic drugs as a first line of defense. Also, consider that medical doctors have a vested interest in giving you advice that promotes drugs.

Most medical schools in the world are heavily funded by the drug industry, which means they have say in the curriculum at these schools. The pharmaceutical companies provide them with drug samples that once given, produce profits not only for the drug companies in future sales, but also produces monetary bonuses and incentives for helping to "share" the product with prospective users. So, when you ask, expect to receive an answer that benefits their overall agenda of profit, not your health.

Chapter Three

WHAT EXACTLY IS
CHIROPRACTIC?

Even though chiropractic has been active since 1895, most people in general still do not understand what chiropractic is or how chiropractic can benefit their overall wellbeing. Most do not realize that chiropractic is a drugless, nonsurgical system of health care. It is by far one of the safest forms of health care available today, far safer than surgery, drugs or chemical treatments. Many people have falsely believed the untrue statements and false rumors concerning chiropractic rather than experiencing chiropractic for themselves.

I've long held the belief that if everyone was checked for vertebral subluxation and adjusted on a regular basis from the time of birth until burial the world would be a better, safer and healthier place to live. Chiropractic care has been commonly known to free people from back and neck pains. While that is true, chiropractic is much more than that. Research has proven that chiropractic helps your hormonal system, respiratory system, and digestive system.

Furthermore, it helps the heart and lungs to perform better by clearing the channels for the brain to freely send messages to the organs without interference. Chiropractic helps to establish homeostasis in the body making everything function better. For those who already understand the fundamentals of chiropractic, some of what you will read will serve as a needed refresher. For those who are new to chiropractic, you will discover one of the greatest health and wellness discoveries of our time, without the use of drugs or surgery.

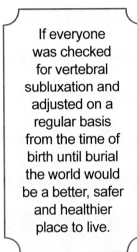

If everyone was checked for vertebral subluxation and adjusted on a regular basis from the time of birth until burial the world would be a better, safer and healthier place to live.

Is Natural Better?

In the past few decades, The United States has become enamored with the concept of natural and "all natural," especially when it refers to food products or topical products such as lotion, soap, and ointments. The idea is that if a product is natural, then it is better for consumption and use. The whole idea of something being unnatural lends to the concept that it was grown, fed, reared or exposed to products or environments that compromised its natural state. For example, many grocery store chains market their cattle meats as being grass fed.

As a child, this marketing strategy would have sounded a bit silly as nearly all cows were grass fed. That was the norm. Over time, big food corporations realized that they could crush their competition if they could produce meat quicker, larger, and cheaper. With that, they began to use unnatural ways of raising their cattle. They would use drugs such as steroids and growth hormones to speed up the process of development, at times cutting the process in half. Their cattle would mature in half the time, often weighing twice the weight.

While this may have been good for business, this model wreaked havoc on the body, as every toxic chemical that went into the cattle became a resident inside of the person that consumed it. Some of these food-borne chemicals have been known to cause or instigate diseases, such as cancer, diabetes, and hypertension. From this perspective, it may be easy to understand why natural is better. Purchasing food that is harvested responsibly and ethically may initially cost more, but will ensure more vibrant health while slashing medical expenses.

Using the same thought process to look at health care, is chiropractic care better than other forms of treatment? The first thing to understand is that chiropractic is an "all natural" health care procedure. It uses specific and strategic spinal adjustment techniques to correct misalignments in the spine often referred to as subluxation, helping your body to heal naturally. The primary purpose of adjustments is to help restore proper function to the nervous system. Once that is done the body can heal itself, as it was intended to do.

The chiropractic adjustment can only be properly performed by professionally trained specialists called chiropractors. This is important in that there are people around the world who may try to perform chiropractic procedures but have not been trained to do so. That could be dangerous. Dr. Lewis had a lovely home in Panama City, Panama a few years ago. He would travel from New England to Panama one to two times monthly. At the time, he was averaging more than one hundred thousand miles a year on airplanes, traveling throughout the world on business. Often when he landed in Panama and settled into his home, the very first thing that he wanted was to get an adjustment to relieve himself of fatigue, back and neck tightness caused by sitting for long periods of time.

Panama does not have many trained chiropractors. Because of this, there are many "gypsy," untrained chiropractors performing adjustments on people and getting paid well. Dr. Lewis was one of those people that was worked on by an imposter. Fortunately, he was not hurt. However, once he realized that the gentleman that was working on him was not professionally trained, he immediately stopped using his services. Lewis was fortunate. There are others who have been severely hurt by allowing someone who was untrained to practice on them.

Some people were left paralyzed and others had near fatal occurrences. So, the first thing that you should always know is that unless a person has chiropractic training don't let them put their hands on you. Chiropractic literally means "done with hands." Chiropractors use their hands or at times specially designed instruments to apply a controlled, sudden force to a spinal joint. In doing so, they can position the joint in its proper place, relieving the nerves of pressure and releasing the flow of energy and transmitted signals to and from the body.

The chiropractic adjustment can only be properly performed by professionally trained specialists called chiropractors.

The Case for Chiropractic

When I was a child, there were medical doctors just as there are today. The difference though, is that then medical doctors were committed to helping to find a way to bring about healing without the use of drugs and surgery. 'One of the first duties of the physician is to educate the masses not to take medicine.' This is a quote by William Osler, and MD who years ago was one of the founding professors of Johns Hopkins Hospital. Drugs and surgery were a last option, a final resort. In today's culture, drugs and surgery tend to be the first line of defense. What makes that problem enormously concerning is that the drugs and surgery are not always foolproof. In fact, they often make things worse.

Yet, in a world that is infused with "drug consciousness," it can be difficult to persuade the average person just how detrimental this chemically laden path can be. Many people ardently defend living a drugged lifestyle. There are thousands of drug commercials shown all over the

United States daily, on television, the internet, and even through social networking ads. No matter where you go you can find this system of brainwashing doing its job on the masses.

Most of the major medical schools in the United States are funded by the pharmaceutical companies and those same companies dictate their curricula which expressly trains new MD's to always assign a drug to every symptom. The situation is out of control, and people are continuing to get sicker and sicker. Now more than ever chiropractic is needed to address the problems of sickness in our world using a drugless approach. Over the past 3 ½ decades I've adjusted thousands of people. Many of them have, of their own admission, stated that after their adjusted they were cured of:

Migraine Headaches
Chronic Back Pain
Ear Infections, especially in young children
Arthritis
Asthma
Scoliosis
High Blood Pressure
Severe Neck Pain

There are countless times, that I remember my patients, who were recommended to have emergency surgical procedures, no longer needed to have surgery after getting regular adjustments. Patients who were diagnosed with improper function in their organs were restored to healthy and proper function. In pregnant mothers, chiropractic adjustments eased normal pains associated with childbearing and helped to promote overall healthy pregnancies. These are only a few of the many benefits that chiropractic care delivers. If chiropractic is so great, then why isn't the entire world getting adjusted? The truth is that not enough people are sharing the word about chiropractic. Honestly, chiropractors and those receiving chiropractic care must do a more effective job in helping to spread the word about chiropractic.

The claims that I've mentioned above are from the mouths of my patients. Sometimes medical professionals and critics of natural healthcare will question the claims of the people whose health have improved because of chiropractic care. This is strange to me, in that if anyone should know whether something is working, it should be the person receiving the care. Often, critics claim that chiropractic does not back its claims with scientific proof. Again, this makes little sense because the problem is never under the burden of proof but only the solution or the cure.

If you go to a medical doctor and tell him or her that you have the problem of a throbbing headache, you cannot prove scientifically that your head is hurting, yet surely you know it is hurting. They don't require you to prove your head hurts before they prescribe heavy duty medication. You don't have to prove your problem exists. For the most part, they take you at your word. The same thing goes for whiplash, back pain, neck pain, or aching joints. You don't have to prove any of those things before you get help. If you could not walk straight, yet after a series of adjustments you can now walk straight and posture-perfect, that shouldn't have to be verified by scientific research. The proof is rather obvious.

However, there are still some people that require certain proof for them to believe in the value of a natural technique. Interestingly, most drugs that are prescribed do not have a foolproof system to determine the outcome of its usefulness for every person that uses it. Yet, people continue to use the drug. Every human being is different and will take to things differently than another person will.

Some people may use the drug oxycontin for severe pain and it may reduce pain for one person. Another person may take the same drug and become addicted. One might take the drug and die. Each of these three scenarios had different after-effects, yet this drug is backed by scientific research. The point is that chiropractic proof is based both on research and personal experience. But one cannot rule out personal experience, because experience is another form of valid proof.

When I nearly died from the spider bite, I knew firsthand that I wouldn't be alive without getting regularly adjusted and without the help of Dr. Dawn Stranges who provided energy and spiritual healing practices on me. I know where I was physically and spiritually when I was bitten and where I am now after treatment and care. My results are based on my experiences. If I waited for science to verify whether the procedures were going to be authorized and approved, I'd be dead. I'm alive now and continually getting better. However, for the person who needs research to believe, consider these facts about chiropractic.

Decreases Blood Pressure

A 2007 study in the Journal of Human Hypertension looked at a group of patients with high blood pressure. Half of the patients received an atlas adjustment, the other half received a mock adjustment. The decrease in blood pressure was so dramatic in the patients who received actual adjustments that the researchers wrote that it "is similar to that seen by giving two different anti-hypertensive agents simultaneously." In fact, 85% of the study patients had improvement after the very first adjustment.

Reduces Stress

In 2011, a team of Japanese researchers studied 12 men who were given chiropractic adjustments and examined PET scan images and blood chemistry to examine the effect that chiropractic has on the autonomic nervous system. After receiving a chiropractic neck adjustment, patients had altered brain activity in the parts of the brain responsible for pain processing and stress reactions. They also had significantly reduced cortisol levels, indicating decreased stress. Participants also reported lower pain scores and a better quality of life after treatment.

Relieves Asthma Symptoms

A 2013 study reported that chiropractic adjustments were effective at increasing lung functioning, and some recent research shows that chiropractic care can help reduce the symptoms of asthma in some children.

These are just a few of the researched benefits of chiropractic. There are many more.

Consider Chiropractic First

Dr. Lewis' father had seen a back surgeon and it was recommended that he have surgery. Dr. Lewis warned his father against the dangers of surgery and expressed that he had many friends who had the same surgery and yet they were still in pain. He told him that many of those types of surgeries were unsuccessful. He told his father, "Dad you really need to begin seeing a chiropractor regularly. I really believe that if you do, your back pain will be corrected over time." His dad was impatient as he was dealing with some pretty major pains from a lower back disc shift. While Lewis realized that his father was dealing with some pretty uncomfortable pain, he also understood that the problem that he was dealing with would not be an easy fix for the surgeon.

The surgeon made strong claims that the back surgery would alleviate the problem and that his back pain would go away. Lewis told his father that he should give chiropractic a try first. He explained in detail what chiropractic was and how it would help him without drugs or surgery. Like most people, his dad believed the medical doctor, since conventional medicine is widely accepted as the standard. He scheduled the surgery, was operated on and was unable to walk for nearly a month after. His doctor told him that everything would be fine and that he would heal without incident. That was not true.

His father's back became worse than it was before. In fact, he argued that the pain that he felt prior to getting surgery was minimal compared to his present back pain. Even months after the surgery, he began to experience excruciating back pain to the point that it was nearly unbearable. With that, he called his son, Dr. Lewis and asked him to recommend a good chiropractor in the area. He did, and he began to regularly get adjustments. While on one hand Lewis was pleased that his father was getting adjustments, it somewhat made him disappointed that his dad would only consider chiropractic after the surgeon made his back worsen.

Unfortunately, many people consider chiropractic as a cure-all to correct a botched job after a surgeon created more problems. The rule of thumb is to consider chiropractic first, not as a last resort. If, however, you consider it as a last resort, it's still better than not considering it at all. However, it is easier, quicker, and less painful to correct the core cause of the pain than to see if scar tissue and further misalignment can be reversed. Chiropractors are trained to locate subluxations and properly adjust the spine. And the sooner that one becomes a regular patient, the sooner that they will be able to receive the healing associated with regular care.

Lewis' dad began to become better after getting adjustments, even after his first surgery. He started walking again. The pain was reduced significantly. And he began to see himself living out a healthy life again, for someone in his early eighties.

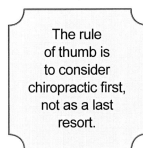

The rule of thumb is to consider chiropractic first, not as a last resort.

Lewis' mother, who didn't believe in chiropractic, began to influence his dad against getting the regular adjustments. She'd say, "You know that they aren't helping you at all. It's all in your mind. You really need to stop going to them and wasting your time." With misguided advice, he stopped going to the chiropractor all together. Within one month's time the pain came back again. This time more severely.

He went back to his doctor to get checked as to why his back was in such pain only to discover that he would be recommended a second surgery. Again, Lewis advised his dad not to have the surgery. He reasoned that "If the first surgery didn't work then what would make you believe that a second one would be any different?" He received a second surgery anyway. This time is was different. It was worse. He ended up with a constant a chronic aching that lasted nearly all day. Prior to the second surgery his pain was intermittent. But now the pain never stopped. The doctor recommended Oxycodone for the pain and Percocet. Lewis remembered his father vomiting, feeling nauseous, and losing nearly thirty pounds as a result. Because of his allergic reaction to the medicine, the doctor kept adjusting the medication, swapping drugs trying to find which pain medication would be the proper fit. So, the only way that he could manage his pain was to take pills

You can't listen to people's negative talk when it comes to your health.

every day. Strangely, the doctor offered a third surgery to correct the two previous mistakes, however this time he offered to perform the surgery without charge. He declined the offer, and to this day lives in chronic pain.

The point is that many people are talked out of doing the right thing, getting regular adjustments from a chiropractor before tragedy strikes. And even if tragedy strikes, getting the advice of a chiropractic doctor first is generally the best choice that you could make. Lewis learned from this experience that you can't listen to people's negative talk when it comes to your health. If you are in pain you are the one that will live with it if you choose not to receive the appropriate help. So, you should make the quality decision to receive the help you need despite what the pessimists have to say.

I've heard critics say of chiropractic that they use sales and marketing tactics and over-treatment even of children and babies. Isn't this true more so of the entire medical industry? No one thinks it to be strange when parents are marketed vaccinations for their newborn babies? No one thinks it to be strange when drug companies use television commercials and other visual advertisements to scare you into buying their drugs?

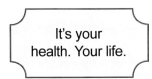

It's your health. Your life.

Yet people think it is unethical to use marketing tactics to help educate people on why they need to choose natural healing as an alternative to traditional medicine. Some people say that chiropractic offers "too good to be true" claims of treating nearly anything with spinal adjustments, including diseases. My simple question to you is: what if it is? What if chiropractic can treat various ailments in the body? Is it worth risking? You decide. It's your health. Your life.

Chapter Four

IF YOU CAN'T READ IT
DON'T EAT IT

There are many things that one should do to maintain optimal health. However, there are many do nots that one should avoid as well. The obvious or more commonly understood "do nots" such as excessive drinking, cigarette smoking, and drug use are ones that many people know to avoid. Most people understand that cigarette smoking may lead to cancer and that it adversely affects the lungs. In fact, cigarette packages clearly state the negative side effects of smoking. It even lets pregnant women know how smoking can cause harm to their unborn child.

Excessive drinking often leads to cirrhosis of the liver. Using addictive drugs can lead to uncertain death. These are the "knowns" that people generally know to avoid. If they choose to abuse these things, they do so at their own risk. But they've been duly informed on the major risk factors these things pose to their health. The serious problem is when you are using a product that you don't even know may be slowly killing you; consuming a harmful toxin that you've not been informed about. That is the case with these seven things that you will discover in this book. It's true that it's not too late to reclaim your health.

However, trying to get your health back, (not realizing that some food companies are working even harder on keeping you sick and addicted) may become counterproductive. It is often attributed to Sir Francis Bacon as having said, "Knowledge is power." I believe that is true. Just think about the reverse. If knowledge is power, then ignorance is surely death. Since this book is all about life and how to live life to the fullest, we felt that it was appropriate to inform you about a few things that may surprise you of which you may not be aware, so that you can be armed with the knowledge to protect your family and what goes into your body. What you and your family eats forms the body and tissues of their bodies.

The problem, however, is that you may have no idea what may be killing you. The reason you don't know is because you cannot read it. Wait, don't get offended. That isn't because you are illiterate. I know you can read, you're reading this book. You see, most whole foods you can read easily. Most natural ingredients you can read. But the things that are bringing great harm to

> If knowledge is power, then ignorance is surely death.

you are actual chemicals and deadly toxins; things used in paints, petroleum, paint thinners, household cleaners, and lab experiments. These additives were never meant for human consumption. Because of that, it's incredibly difficult to read what it is, as they weren't meant to be easily understood by the average, or even above average person.

The Food and Drug Administration (FDA) approves the use of many of these products as long as they do not have large doses. This leads me to believe that there may be a conspiratorial effort within the government to at least keep you perpetually sick, as sickness and disease garner huge profits. Plainly put, sickness and disease are huge business. So, as you continue to read we'll elaborate very briefly about each one of these commonly used additives.

Some of them are for seasonings and flavor. Others just irretrievably break down the body all together. Please take the time to further research each of these later. What you'll discover will be disturbing. But it is far better to know that not to know at all. This chapter is about keeping you abreast of these things that have become widespread and continue to pose health hazards to you and the people that you love. Just remember, if you can't read it don't eat it!

Enemy # 1 – Monosodium Glutamate

Monosodium glutamate, also known as MSG or sodium glutamate is a naturally occurring non-essential amino

> MSG is almost always used in Chinese fast food restaurants.

acid. It is found in cheese and tomatoes. MSG causes a medical condition known as Chinese Restaurant Syndrome. The food industry widely uses MSG to enhance the flavor of food. MSG gives food a savory flavor, often referred to as an "umami" taste, which increases the satisfying flavor in stews, meat soups and a host of snacks and processed foods. MSG is almost always used in Chinese fast food restaurants. Often, they are used even in Chinese restaurants that offer a disclaimer stating otherwise.

People are generally driven by good taste, and there is nothing wrong with that. Since MSG packs in the flavor and helps to enhance the enjoyment of the eating experience, people become somewhat addicted to the taste, thus causing them to always desire the taste. But what's in the taste may be costing your health dearly.

MSG is an excitoxin, which overexcites your blood cells and can cause severe damage or death.

It affects the nervous system.

It can increase the risk of brain damage.

Studies have shown that certain overuse of MSG can trigger learning disabilities in children and adults.

It increases the risk of obesity.

It has been linked to headaches, fatigue and disorientation, tingling and numbness.

It may cause eye damage.

It may cause rapid or fluctuating heartbeat.

It is linked to certain forms of depression.

Affects forty percent of the population.

Part of the problem also is that free glutamic acid is the same neurotransmitter that your brain and nervous system, uses to initiate certain processes in your body. *Abnormal function of glutamate receptors has been linked with certain neurological diseases, such as Alzheimer's disease and Huntington's chorea.*

Enemy # 2 –Trisodium Phosphate

Cold cereals have long been considered a heathy breakfast choice, especially for growing children. Most ingredients boast a full assortment of daily vitamins and nutrients that are needed to help you and your family maintain good health. But what most don't know is that some cereals such as Lucky Charms, Cheerios, and Cinnamon Toast Crunch have been known to add TSP also known as Trisodium Phosphate to their cereals. TSP is not a vitamin or trace mineral. It's not an herb nor a daily essential for the body. Yet, TSP is added to major brand cereals as if it's vital. TSP is not meant for human consumption and is harmful to the body.

TSP can be found in many all-purpose and heavy duty household and commercial cleaning products. If you visit

Home Depot or Lowes Home Improvement stores and check out their deck, wood, and siding cleaners and you'll be sure to find TSP as one of its main ingredients. The Original Deck and Siding Cleaner is a popular brand, as is Simple Green non-solvent cleaner. They both contain TSP. TSP controls and eliminates lead paint dust and is used to clean surfaces to prepare them for painting. That is disgusting.

The U.S. Food and Drug Administration (FDA) does not prohibit the use of this chemical in cereals despite its adverse effect on the body. They claim that it contains a small enough amount of TSP to not cause harm to the body. While that may sound appealing it really doesn't make sense. If that were the case, then the same standard should be used for all prohibited and harmful items. People who use cocaine, methamphetamine, heroine, or hallucinogens aren't given a go pass from the Drug Enforcement Agency if they use minimal amounts. If you use a small amount and get caught, you'll be arrested and charged. If you use a larger portion you'll be arrested and charged.

Small amounts of drugs have a harmful effect on the body, as do chemicals that go into the body. The cereal companies claim that they've used this chemical since the 1950s and it is used as a stabilizer and preservative for the food. They also claim that the small exposure to TSP hasn't caused any harm to anyone. Unfortunately, that isn't true. Moreover, there is no conclusive evidence or research that proves that this chemical is safe to be consumed. Because of that, we take the position that ingesting the active ingredient in paint strippers and strong outdoor cleansers is probably not the best choice for your morning meal.

Remember that most people in the Western world tend to overindulge in pretty much everything. Excess is typically what leads to more problems in the body. For example, the daily limit of trisodium phosphate that is permitted is in the area of 70mg per day. Most Westerners via a hefty junk food daily diet consumes more than 500 mg of TSP each day, placing their health in the danger zone. Excessive intake of TSP may produce:

> An imbalance of minerals that leads to loss of calcium from bone and a calcification of kidneys
> An increased risk of developing osteoporosis

Enemy # 3 –Potassium Nitrate

Potassium Nitrate is one of the key ingredients in an array of assorted products and foods such as toothpaste, gunpowder, agricultural fertilizers and fireworks. It's commonly found in cheese and cured meats such as corned beef, salami, and pepperoni. This preservative, which is commonly called sodium nitrate or saltpeter, wreaks havoc on the body, especially when the body heats up. When this

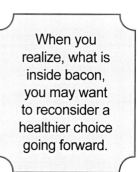

When you realize, what is inside bacon, you may want to reconsider a healthier choice going forward.

happens, it begins to morph into chemical compounds called nitrosamines that have been known to cause toxic effects in various animal species. One of the foods that nitrosamines are abundant in is crispy bacon, a breakfast favorite among so many people. When you realize, what is inside bacon, you may want to reconsider a healthier choice going forward. According to research and studies Potassium Nitrate:

May cause diabetes
May cause Parkinson's Disease
May cause Alzheimer's Disease
Has been known to promote stomach cancer in humans

Enemy # 4 T*rans* Fats

In November 2013, the U.S. Food and Drug Administration made a preliminary determination that trans fats, also known as partially hydrogenated oils, are no longer Generally Recognized as Safe (GRAS) in human food. While this was long considered to be safe (decades prior), artificial trans fats have been linked to several health problems. It is more than likely that much human suffering and early death might have otherwise been averted if trans fats were avoided all together. Naturally occurring trans fats are produced in the intestines of some animals and are passed along to us via the food from these animals, from which we obtain some of our meat and milk products.

70

Artificial trans fats are created using an industrial process that adds hydrogen to liquid vegetable oils to solidify them. This gives the food prepared with trans-fat a desirable taste and texture. But the real reason why restaurants and consumers use trans-fat is because it's cheap, easy to use, inexpensive to produce, and has a nearly eternal shelf life. They can sell it economically and it produces enormous profits in return. Trans fats are so bad that some European countries such as Switzerland and Denmark and even the U.S.A.'s next door neighbor, Canada, has reduced or restricted the use of trans fats in food service establishments. Why would they do that? Scientists have discovered that trans fats raise your bad LDL cholesterol levels and lower your good HDL cholesterol levels. Also, Trans Fats:

Increases your risk of developing heart disease
May cause stroke
Are associated with high risk of developing type 2 diabetes

Furthermore, beware of the labels that say, 0 or ZERO TRANS FAT. Because there has been extensive research on trans fats in the past couple of decades, there is heightened awareness on the subject. With that, many food producers have gotten permission from the FDA that if they have their trans fats levels below a certain percentage in their food (less than 0.5 %), they can label their products as having 0 TRANS FAT. So, it's not true. There are many foods that you can be sure have trans fats in them. The best practice is to either eliminate them from your diet or to begin limiting the amount of these products you consume on a regular basis. Below is an abridged list of some common foods that Trans Fats are found in.

Trans fats are often found in:
Doughnuts
Fast food fried chicken and fried fish
Cakes and pies
Biscuits
Frozen Pizza
Cookies and Crackers
Stick Margarines (I call it the stick of death)
Vegetable Oil Spreads
And a host of boxed processed foods found in the frozen section of your local grocer

Enemy # 5 –Aspartame

For many years, artificial sweeteners have been thought to help obese people maintain healthy weight levels. That is simply untrue. In fact, in many cases artificial sweeteners have been known to cause far more harm to the body than regular sugar. Aspartame is not a natural sweetener in that is does not grow from a plant or vegetable. It is a man-made product. For more than twenty years the FDA refused to approve this chemical as it was unsafe, and all the research trying to prove otherwise was skewed. NutraSweet and Equal are among the most notable brands containing aspartame that market to the consumer as alternatives to sugar products.

They target people with diabetes, people who are overweight, or those who have had a family history of dealing with both. The idea is that if you choose something "other" than sugar, then you will have much better health. There are more than 6,000 products on the market today that contain aspartame. And these products are consumed daily by 100 million people around the globe. Most people do not realize the debilitating effects that this product has on the body. Even more, most do not realize that this artificial sweetener is in so many products:

Chewable vitamins
Sugar-Free cough drops
Tabletop sweeteners for tea and coffee
Most diet and sugar free sodas
And even Yogurt

Worse yet is that through numerous tests on animals and humans, continued use of these sweeteners have been found to cause several complications in the body. Here is a partial list of why artificial sweeteners is not too sweet at all, contributing to:

High cholesterol levels
Sabotage of weight loss efforts
Fluid loss in the body
Migraines
Nausea and vomiting
Change in vision
Abdominal and Joint Pains
Fluctuating Heart Rate

Memory Loss

Produced tumors in animal lab tests

Seizures

Depression

Insomnia

Brain Cancer

Diagnosis of Multiple Sclerosis (MS), due to similar symptoms

Enemy # 6 –High Fructose Corn Syrup

The adage says, "Moderation in all things." This saying was in the works of the Greek poet Hesiod and has become a common favorite phrase amongst people with traditionalist views on life health and spirituality. While that phrase has great meaning and substance, the truth is that most people are not moderate about anything. The United States of America is in the top ten of the most obese countries in the world. Estonia, Lithuania, and Belarus lead the world in alcohol related deaths. Iceland, Estonia and the United States are world leaders for high drug overdoses and drug related deaths.

> The United States of America is in the top ten of the most obese countries in the world.

Just from these few examples, it is clear that people around the world do not always subscribe to the idea of moderation in all things. In fact, many people are overindulgent, excessive, and extreme in their lifestyles. One extreme that is addictive and dangerous is high fructose syrup. In the United States, we eat high doses of sugar, especially in the form of high fructose corn syrup. It's sweeter and cheaper to produce than regular sugar. You can find high fructose syrup in nearly every processed food and sugar-filled drink on the market. The average person consumes nearly 150 pounds of sugar each year.

That's like a person eating their own weight in a year. An average 20-ounce soft drink contains 15 teaspoons of high fructose corn syrup. When anyone consumes sugar in such high doses it becomes toxic. In the chemical process of making high fructose corn syrup, glucose and fructose become separated. When this happens, it turns your body into a fat producing machine in your liver through a process called lipogenesis. This leads to fatty liver which affects nearly 90 million Americans. It is best to avoid high fructose syrup all together. It is found mostly in low quality food. Continued use in high amounts of high fructose corn syrup can lead to:
Type 2 Diabetes
Heart Attacks
Strokes
Cancer
Dementia

Enemy # 7 –BHA and BHT

Is it better for food to spoil or for you to spoil? If I had to choose I'd rather that food spoiled than myself. However, a better idea is to eat food, whole food that is, before it spoils at all. BHA and BHT stands for Butylated hydroxyanisole *(BHA) and Butylated* hydroxytoluene (BHT) are food additives that are used in food products to help prevent foods from spoiling quickly. These chemicals are found in many meats, cereals, crackers, chips, butter and dairy products, chewing gum, beer, many snack foods, pet foods, make-up, lotions and soap, dehydrated potatoes and a host of processed foods.

Although this product received approval from the FDA, they have known it to cause cancer and negatively affect human behavior. It is thought that if one consumes low doses, that he or she will be relatively unaffected by the negative effects. Our position is that regardless of how little poison is in a product, it is still worth staying clear of, especially if a potential side effect happens to be cancer. Under many circumstances scientific words disguise a hidden truth, that the foods containing these hard to pronounce words are often killing you. One person once said, "It is always better to err on the side of caution." I wholeheartedly agree.

Begin the process of making wiser and more life-filled choices regarding your eating. You don't have to change everything overnight. However, to secure a cleaner bill of health you must get started. Start by eliminating a few things and then add to the list. Replace what you eliminate with whole food healthy choices. In time, you will begin to look and feel better than

If it's not food, then don't eat it.

you've ever been. Remember your body wasn't designed to live off chemicals. If it's food and it's not in a foreign language you'll probably be able to pronounce it. If it's not food, then don't eat it.

Chapter Five

BACK TO CHIROPRACTIC

There are a variety of different techniques chiropractors use to care for their patients. In fact, there are a vast amount of ways to analyze, detect and correct vertebral subluxations; far too many to list and discuss here in this book. Therefore, we are just going to comment on a few of the many powerful techniques. What we would like to convey to you is that if you are not getting the desired results that you were hoping for, you may need to find a chiropractor with the technique that aligns best with your body. The point is, do not give up on chiropractic, rather find a technique that works for you.

We believe wholeheartedly that our world will be a whole lot healthier if we all get back to the basic principles of chiropractic and getting checked regularly to ensure that your spine is functioning optimally. As with food and other lifestyle or healthcare choices, there

> Our world will be a whole lot healthier if we all get back to the basic principles of chiropractic and getting checked regularly to ensure that your spine is functioning optimally

are always desired preferences in life. Not everyone likes hotdogs and hamburgers. Some people are allergic to shellfish, others can live without it. In life we come to realize that one size doesn't always fit all. So, let's discover some techniques to find out a best fit for you.

Please be aware that we are not endorsing any one technique or method over another. From our personal research and clinical experience, we have found that all of these techniques work, but may not always work for each person in the same way, nor even for the same person at different times! No two persons on earth are exactly the same. Also, every person may respond differently to certain methods. There are several factors that may vary results, such as age, size, weight, muscular build, athletic ability, and overall state of health and well-being.

Another crucial factor is the severity and chronicity of the spinal condition at the initial time of treatment. For example, if a person's spine is severely degenerated, there is less that can be done by way of chiropractic. However, if there are still some healthy cushions in between the vertebrae, the chiropractor can help immensely to reduce pain through regular adjustments. Many conditions can be improved in the body through early detection of vertebral subluxation.

Each of the following techniques listed are shared with us by chiropractors who have mastered their respective techniques.

Gonstead Technique

By Dr. Tom Potisk, the author of *Whole Health Healing: The Budget Friendly Natural Wellness Bible for All Ages*

In 1982, when I was a student at Palmer College of Chiropractic in Davenport, Iowa, I began to hear a lot of talk about a super-successful chiropractor whose stories sounded practically unbelievable. My fellow students were talking about some man who had a practice so large, attracting people from all over the world, that he had to build a landing strip and airport, adjacent to his clinic for his clients to fly in to. Dr. Clarence Gonstead, from Mount Horeb, WI ran arguably one of the most successful chiropractic clinics in the world, often termed "The Mayo Clinic" equivalent in Chiropractic.

As a student I was learning various chiropractic methods commonly referred to as techniques. Certainly all of the techniques I was learning had benefits for patients. However, the stories of Gonstead captured my attention as a young student. Intrigued by Dr. Gonstead I journey off to meet him face to face, only to discover that he had passed away four years before, in 1978. Thankfully, Dr. Gonstead had taught several chiropractors his unique method, many of whom have mastered this technique.

Larry Troxell, D.C., one of those certified Gonstead instructors, was operating the Troxell Intern Program at his clinic near Davenport.

I applied for this program and was admitted to study under him. For two evenings each week, I would intern with him, watching, learning, assisting and studying how Dr. Troxell perfected his technique, working with his large volume of patients each day. The results that the patients received were outstanding. There were patients with not only musculoskeletal problems but also digestive, circulatory, and respiration issues that received remarkable improvements and miraculous healings. Witnessing that firsthand, impressed me even more with the power of chiropractic healing.

Dr. Gonstead's story is quite noteworthy. He graduated from Palmer College in 1923. The five plus decades of his practice were some of the most turbulent times in the chiropractic profession. Many chiropractors struggled to sustain small one or two room offices, often in their homes. There was no insurance coverage for chiropractic. Many states didn't even have a system to license chiropractors, which caused hundreds of chiropractors to go to jail as they accused them of practicing medicine without a license. The overall public perception of the profession was negative.

Getting referrals from medical doctors was extremely rare, as most medical doctors did not understand what chiropractors actually did or how they would fit into the scheme of the health profession. Many of the hardships were brought about by the well-organized plan by the American Medical Association to discredit, contain, and ultimately eliminate the chiropractic profession. This was a real conspiracy that did not end until a lawsuit was filed in the United States Supreme Court, when a Supreme Court Justice ordered the AMA to stop their illegal and unjustified boycott in 1984. Those thirty or so years prior to this landmark case marked the darkest decades in chiropractic's history.

In the spirit of the darkness there was still a bright light shining at Gonstead's clinic. While the persecution against the profession was happening all over the country, Dr. Gonstead, seemed almost oblivious to the attacks and stayed completely focused on building a practice that attracted people from literally all over the world to the tiny village of Mount Horeb, Wisconsin, with a population of only 1700 to 1900 people during his heyday. Gonstead would treat 300 to 450 people daily.

Many patients came to Gonstead as a last resort, unable to get help anywhere else. There were so many people, that it caused the need to construct a landing strip juxtaposed to his clinic, as the infrastructure in Mount Horeb could not sufficiently accommodate the influx of patients. Chiropractors from all over the United States took notice of his remarkable success and began asking Gonstead to teach them his technique. From that, the Gonstead Method was developed and taught to practitioners all over the world.

The uniqueness of the Gonstead Chiropractic Method is multifaceted. It is a full spine, hands-on method of specifically finding and adjusting the primary spinal subluxation. It uses several criteria to pinpoint the subluxation including analysis with a full spine weight-bearing x-ray, a heat sensitive instrument, i.e. Nervoscope scan of the spine, visualization of spinal posture, static and motion digital palpation of vertebral movement, and careful history taking. Once found, the primary subluxation is then carefully and specifically adjusted on one of several unique, specialized adjusting tables perfected by Dr. Gonstead.

The goal is to apply the specific adjustment with very little force causing a very comfortable experience for the patient. Specific adjusting is highly effective in releasing nerve interference, so the body can utilize its God-given natural healing abilities. This is principled chiropractic at its best. Prior to becoming a chiropractor, Dr. Gonstead was a mechanical engineer, in which he used specific lessons learned to develop and perfect his methods in chiropractic. In my own practice, I've used the Gonstead Method and have had tremendous success, building one of the largest practices in my area. Of his high-volume practice Gonstead once said, "I did not build this clinic for myself; I built it for Chiropractic."

To learn more about Gonstead's legacy and life you can visit www.gonstead.com.

Applied Kinesiology

Applied Kinesiology was developed in 1963 by Dr. George Goodheart from Detroit, Michigan. Dr. Goodheart took on a case of a teenage boy who had tried several different medical disciplines including other chiropractors, osteopaths, physical therapists, physiatrists and orthopedists to help cure his condition. This young man suffered from pain and postural malformation of his shoulder blade with a condition diagnosed as a winged scapula. His scapula bone stuck out and would not stay where it was designed to, serving the purpose for which it was created.

Interestingly, until recently, most doctors of all healing arts believed that most musculoskeletal conditions were the result of muscle strains and ligament strains which resulted in spasmed or over-contracted muscles frequently referred to by lay people and health care practitioners as tight or tense muscles. Corrective measures were usually employed to reduce spasms. Considering that, it was quite understandable why this young man wanted to be checked by Dr. Goodheart. The doctor's first attempt was to relax the spastic muscles that were keeping this young man's shoulder out of position.

All of the other doctors that he visited tried this method, but it did not work. Dr. Goodheart eventually determined that what was pulling the shoulder blade out of position was not a spastic muscle, but was rather a weak muscle. He found that the supraspinatus muscle in the boy's back was particularly weak. He developed a system to test the strength of the muscles manually and to manually correct the muscle weakness by contacting certain points on the spine. Some of these points are considered to be similar to acupuncture points, which might be called acupressure points. Some were reflex points, called Chapman's reflexes, which had previously been determined by an osteopathic doctor, Dr. Chapman.

Dr. Goodheart found that by stimulating and/or sedating some of these points manually he could successfully straighten the boy out by strengthening the supraspinatus muscle, which Dr. Goodheart had determined through his manual muscle testing was particularly weak. This technique of testing muscles and strengthening weak ones to bring appropriate posture and spinal alignment served to improve the patient's overall state.

In essence, Applied Kinesiology is both a diagnostic and therapeutic tool.

Sacro Occipital Technique (S.O.T)
By Dr. Liam Miller, Saint Paul, MN

Founded in 1925 by Major Bertrand De Jarnette, who was both an osteopath and a chiropractor, Sacro Occipital Technique is a method of chiropractic based upon the scientific finding that normal respiratory function activates cerebrospinal fluid flow between the

> Applied Kinesiology is both a diagnostic and therapeutic tool.

lower end of the nervous system (the Sacrum) and the upper end (the Occiput). Cerebrospinal fluid flow is very important to the function of our bodies because it bathes the spinal cord and nerve roots exiting the cord. This anatomical chamber, the "dura mater" that surrounds the spinal cord, houses the cerebrospinal fluid flow and assists with appropriate nerve communication system between the brain and every part of the human body.

Major went beyond the basic spinal adjustment and developed methods of correcting the cranium, pelvis, extremities and organs. This study brought about a system of adjusting various patterns in the body, not just single body parts. The most significant pattern was the relationship between the sacrum and occiput (which became the name of the technique).

Dr. Liam Miller is a third-generation chiropractor who practices S.O.T. Miller shares:
"Coming from a rich chiropractic history, and trained in S.O.T., when caring for my patients, I find myself paying a significant amount of attention to the cerebrospinal fluid flow (CSF) and how it's flowing." The CSF flow needs to be as free as possible in order for the mental impulses to travel optimally from the brain down to the sacrum, and back. S.O.T. practitioners focus on balancing the structural relationship between the sacrum and the occiput (base of the skull). Care is directed toward getting the sacrum rocking freely enough to sufficiently pump the CSF back up to the brain.

Many people notice in their photographs that their head frequently tilts in one direction or the other. S.O.T., practitioners direct their care at helping to level the patient's head, placing it in better alignment and communication with the sacrum. "With S.O.T. an attempt is made to align the occiput (base of the skull) into the right position to actively balance the pressure of CSF and allow the brain to float like a bobber within the cranial vault. Care is also designed to get the cranial bones flexing and moving properly to facilitate the CSF flow.

S.O.T. practitioners sometimes use wedge shaped blocks for adjusting the pelvis and spine. While many chiropractic patients enjoy the cracking sound that occurs during a manual adjustment of the spine, some patients are fearful of the cracking sound when manual adjustments are made to the vertebrae. People who feel this way are usually delighted to find out their spine can be adjusted using these S.O.T. blocking procedures without ever experiencing a cracking sound which is merely an audible release of a joint space.

Pre- and post-blocking procedures are done, and specific indicators are evaluated before proceeding to either gentle cranial adjustments or C.M.R.T. (Chiropractic Manipulative Reflex Therapy) of the visceral system. I consider CMRT (Chiropractic Manipulation Reflex Technique) as a useful guide to the vagus nerves activity between the organs and the brain.

Chiropractors who practice S.O.T. will often extensively study craniopathy within S.O.T. Craniopathy opens the chiropractors up to another world of adjustments above the atlas (C1, the top bone in the neck, the most freely movable vertebra of our spinal column). Indicators and reflexes found through the entire body are used in S.O.T. and help provide the doctor and patient a better sense of certainty. S.O.T. allows the whole body, including the organs to be addressed.

Early on in S.O.T.'s development, (from 1931 to 1940), Dr. Major De Jarnette only accepted patients who did not respond to care under other chiropractors.

If you've only had your "problem area" adjusted by a chiropractor and if you have the same adjustment at each and every visit without satisfactory results, perhaps you'd like to explore the world of chiropractic further and you may discover every chiropractor practices a little different approach to the performance of their art.

Atlas Orthogonal Chiropractic Technique
By Dr. Andrea Paporto

Dr. Andrea Paporto, Poughkeepsie, New York, a specialist in this technique recalls how she was introduced to this method and how she became a master of this technique learning from the creator of this technique, Dr. Roy Sweat. Dr. Paporto has personally adjusted my spine for the past decade. I am blessed to be associated with such a fine chiropractor. Dr. Paporto recalls, "When I was 25 years old, I suffered a low back injury and it was recommended that I have back surgery. The surgeon told me that after surgery, it would not be a good idea for me to ever get pregnant."

"At 25 years old I wasn't comfortable with settling for never having children. At that time, I found a chiropractor who explained how chiropractic is a system of healthcare and through a series of full spine adjustments, I would be back on my feet. The full spine adjustments worked for me and with that I decided that I too wanted to become a chiropractor. Nearly one month before leaving for school I had a severe whiplash injury and head trauma. This injury caused me to suffer from severe migraine headaches. As time went on the headaches worsened and within a year I had a constant migraine that never went away - it just fluctuated in intensity."

"At that point, I became desperate. I saw 17 doctors in a three-month period of time, many of which were chiropractors. The chiropractic technique that prevented me from having lower back surgery was not helping me with my migraines. Having moved my family from New York to Georgia to study at Life University and taking on tens of thousands of dollars in school debt, my condition worsened. I became so sick that I couldn't attend classes. My classmates knew me as the student with chronic migraines. I'd chosen a path to help people through chiropractic, to help reduce and eliminate people's pain, yet I could not help my self."

"One day, I met a group of students who were studying the Atlas Orthogonal chiropractic technique with Dr. Roy Sweat. Dr. Sweat operated a clinic in Atlanta and some students decided to take me to his office because they were very confident he would be able to help me. The pain was so unbearable that I was unable to drive. If I even saw sunlight, I'd get really dizzy and nauseous. My balance and walking were off. It came to the point where I didn't even believe that I'd live much longer in that condition. While I do not remember actually walking into the clinic, I'll never forget what happened once I was inside."

"Dr. Sweat adjusted me with the Atlas Orthogonal table mounted instrument. After the adjustment, I began crying, not because I had immediate results, but because I didn't feel anything. For nearly ten minutes, I just laid there crying, not feeling anything, and not feeling as if there were any other options for me. At this point, I just wanted to leave the office and figure out something that would possibly work for me. Dr. Sweat came back into the room and asked me to sit up. I sat up quickly because I wanted to go. It was then that I realized the pain in my head was gone. For the first time in three months I was able to change positions quickly without putting counter pressure on my head."

"Before, I could feel my heartbeat in my head, as if my head was going to split open from the pain. That pain was no longer there. The pain level had gone from a 10 being the worst, to just a 3. I wanted to know what this man had done to my neck. That was the beginning of the rest of my life. From that day forward, I started to learn the Atlas Orthogonal Technique. As a student I spent every free moment I had in Dr. Sweat's office watching him treat patients. Both myself and Dr. Sweat's patients realized that if he was willing to take you as a patient, you were going to get well."

"Dr. Sweat trained at Palmer College in the 50's, where he learned and practiced hand adjusting and spent decades working and teaching atlas adjusting by hand. He realized that no two people were able to deliver the same adjustment. He believed that it was important to make the adjustment to the atlas vertebra a uniform correction so that people could receive the same adjustment even if it came from different doctors. He taught that with hand adjusting there are 211 things that can be done differently. With the table mounted instrument there are less then 10 things a doctor can do differently. Using his table assisted instrument greatly increased the reproducibility of the correction."

"Consider the atlas the first link in the chain. When the atlas is level, or in the orthogonal position, the human body is in balance and the head is positioned in the center of the feet. When the atlas is off center, the head goes off center, the spine shifts to support the weight of the head, thereby creating biomechanical stresses and strains throughout the spine. When the atlas

> With hand adjusting there are 211 things that can be done differently.

is in the orthogonal or neutral position the rest of the spinal vertebra come into better alignment allowing the spine to heal itself."

In my years of practice I have had the privilege of adjusting 1,000's of patients and seeing similar results as seen in Dr. Roy's clinic. I have built one of the largest upper cervical practices in the country based solely on results.

One of the things I am most proud of, is, I have been able to meet and assist Dr. Timothy Schaub in his journey to health and wellness through the use of the Atlas Orthogonal chiropractic technique.
In the words of Dr. Roy Sweat, "God Bless Atlas Orthogonal and God Bless Chiropractic!"

Note: Dr. Andrea Paporto is the Atlas Orthogonal Chiropractor of the year 2018

Network Spinal Care By Dr. Todd Stein, Ithaca, New York

"Any sufficiently advanced technology is indistinguishable from magic."
—Aurthur C. Clarke

Network Spinal Care (NSC) is an evolution of chiropractic science. Developed since the early 1980's, and still being developed today by Dr. Donald Epstein,

A Network Spinal Care practitioner typically uses very light pressure on specific parts of your spine.

NSC has evolved into an extremely specific system of care that elicits an enhanced state of self-awareness in the Central Nervous System, which in turn creates a more efficiently self-correcting nervous system and spine.

Instead of adjusting or aligning your spine through forceful manipulation, a Network Spinal Care practitioner typically uses very light pressure on specific parts of your spine (your neck and tailbone in most cases). The pressure causes a shift in the self-assessment of the Central Nervous System, which in turn generates self-correcting behaviors in the spine, including respiratory changes, wave-like motion of musculature, and changes to the spinal structural holding patterns. Immediate tension release, body and mind relaxation, and a return of available energy to the patient are the usual outcomes.

No twisting, popping, or cracking is necessary for this style of subluxation correction. Even on the very first visit, immediate global changes to spinal tension patterns, and spinal behavior are elicited. These are observed and measured by the practitioner, but more importantly, they are very often felt by the patient. The most common reports from practice members upon sitting up from their first Network Spinal Entrainment include:

"I feel lighter"
"I can breathe again!"
"I am so relaxed."

"I'm sitting up straighter!"
"How did you DO that?"

When I first met Dr. Epstein in 1996, he posited some very profound questions to the audience that he was speaking to:

"How do you know that the adjustment you just delivered to the spine produced a positive change in the nervous system? Are you taking it just on faith? Or do you have a specific analysis that lets you know for sure?"

And my favorite: "What does a healthy, vibrant, energized spine feel like? How does it behave?"
I realized that I had no idea! And without the end goal in mind, we can never get to the destination. I was intrigued enough to learn more.

While working as an Upper Cervical Specific chiropractor, Dr. Epstein took some of the most successful techniques of chiropractic, including Upper Cervical Specific, Gonstead, Pierce-Stillwagon technique, Logan Basic, Toftness, Sacro-Occipital Technique, and others, and searched for where these methods agreed, and how they could be used in such a way TOGETHER to produce the best outcome for the PATIENT. This line of inquiry eventually led to the method of Network Spinal Care that is being taught worldwide today.

"Give a man a fish and you feed him for a day. Teach a man to fish and you feed him for a lifetime."
—Chinese Proverb

> Distortions in spinal function all relate back to the function of the nerves, and the nerve function can be distorted by many kinds of stress: physical injuries, mental and emotional stressors, and chemical toxicity.

Modern chiropractors are taught to feel for distortions and misalignments in the spine, and to adjust the bones to produce more motion. If we follow the basic logic of how our bodies work, it is clear that brain activity is transmitted through our nerves, and the nerve signals control the tension and activity in our muscles (and other organs). It is the muscle activity that coordinates the alignment and pressure in the spinal bones. Therefore, distortions in spinal function all relate back to the function of the nerves, and the nerve function can be distorted by many kinds of stress: physical injuries, mental and emotional stressors, and chemical toxicity.

The Network Spinal Care method gives the practitioner the tools he or she needs to accurately assess the tension in the spinal cord and nerves, and to apply forces that enhance sub-conscious self-assessment, resulting in an automatic self-correction of the spinal misalignments.

With repetition of the care, the patient becomes more aware of the process, as well as more adept and efficient at the skill of stress management and self-correction. More importantly, a stress free nervous system has more energy, and can handle more 'bandwidth' of information that "runs the show" of our health on every level: immune responses, digestive health, cardiovascular function, etc., etc.

When the author of this book, Dr. Tim, first came to me 10 years ago, he was truly barely alive. He was bent over and walking with two canes, with just enough energy in his system to power the basic functions of survival. A man who had captained the largest chiropractic practice in Syracuse for decades, been a body builder, and a lifelong seeker of health, had been reduced to a shell of his former self.

His muscles felt like they were in rigor mortis, and his joints seemed fused together. Not from some horrible accident, but from a spider bite. A toxin to the CNS cut him down and robbed him of his powerful life. There was no way to adjust his vertebrae, short of using a jackhammer.

Over the next few years, through the gentle application of NSC, energy started to flow through his spinal cord, suspending the extreme defense that his system had erected, and he slowly but surely began to improve. Breath returned, muscles unwound, his spine elongated, becoming increasingly erect, and he slowly began to be able to see patients again. He is now as busy as he wants to be in practice and has created a worldwide educational platform that is empowering hundreds of doctors toward greater practice success, and more fulfilling lives with ChiroSushi.

For more information on Network Spinal Care point your browser to:
www.epienergetics.com or www.wiseworldseminars.com

Dr. Todd Stein
Ithaca, NY
Doctodd.healing@gmail.com

Other Techniques

Activator is another popular low force technique that employs a system of spinal analysis. It incorporates the use of a spring-loaded instrument called an Activator. Again, chiropractic was born in America and this form of care arose in the early 1970's from Red Wing Falls, MN (where Red Wing Boots are manufactured). This technique is highly appreciated by patients who are afraid of having their bones and joints manually manipulated.

Neuro Emotional Technique (NET) – This technique was developed by Dr. Scott Walker. Prior to studying chiropractic Dr. Walker practiced traditional psychotherapy for a number of years. After practicing chiropractic, he noticed that a small percentage of his clients did not respond to his care as well as he would have liked them to respond. He felt that this was due to emotional blockages that were keeping the stress in their nervous systems.

Dr. Walker devised an effective system drawing from his knowledge of psychology and chiropractic that identifies stressors locked in the body that prevent ideal form and function. NET employs muscle testing to assess the stressors and determine the most effective means to release them, ushering in greater health.

There are many other methods that I did not mention here. There are also hundreds of methods being developed everyday all over. The main thing is to find the method that is correct for you. If you need help in finding out which method is best for you, just email me and I will gladly respond. I can be reached via email at: doctorsofthefuture@gmail.com.

Chapter Six

LIFE'S A MISSION

If there's one thing that I've learned in life it is this: the value of life has far more to do with what you can give that what you can attain. I've lived life for quite some time now, and I've enjoyed the pleasure of having many things in life. I've lived in fine homes, driven fine cars, worn quality clothing, eaten incredible food, and traveled to some of the most beautiful places in the world. None of those things are bad at all. In fact, they were really all good. I wouldn't trade the life that I've lived for anything. God has blessed me and for that I am grateful.

However, after you've experienced such things in life and enjoyed such pleasures, the soul often yearns for something more-something greater. For me, that something greater began

> If there's one thing that I've learned in life it is this: the value of life has far more to do with what you can give that what you can attain.

with the need to give back. I've always been a giver and always given to philanthropic organizations, both in New York and Nationally. I've given countless adjustments to patients who could not afford chiropractic care. Giving wasn't a struggle for me at all. As I became more spiritually exposed, I became open to missions. I wanted to give of myself in a way that I hadn't before. That is when this great opportunity opened up for me.

Dominican Republic

My friend, Dr. Aaron Lewis, has traveled all over the world to more countries than I can recite. One day in the spring of 2014, he called me and asked would I and Dr. Dawn be available to join him on a mission trip to Dominican Republic. I had never been to the Dominican Republic before. My interest was roused immediately. He shared with me that he would be traveling with some other volunteer workers from his church in Glastonbury, CT and that he needed chiropractors and other health providers to join him.

During that time, I had been dealing with some health challenges resulting from my previous sickness from the spider bite and thought to myself, one hand that it might be a good idea to get away and be refreshed. A change of venue couldn't do any harm. Another thought was I wasn't sure if I'd be able to treat hundreds, perhaps thousands of precious people. If I was going to go, I wanted to make sure that I would be able to give my total self to the cause. I talked it over with Dr. Dawn, weighed all of the options, and committed to go. That was one of one the best decisions I've ever made.

We flew out of Syracuse with connection flights in New York headed to Dominican in October 2014. I didn't know exactly what Dominican was like; but was excited about this grand opportunity to serve. I had heard about Chiro Missions led by chiropractors throughout the world. I've never gone with them, but I did know that they would invite nearly a hundred chiropractors to go to designated countries in South America, the Caribbean, and Europe and would adjust thousands of people over a week or so. This trip didn't have a thousand chiropractors. I was the only one. There was only about ten of us in all that went down.

There were some church Elders, an attorney, an accountant, a Christian businessman and his wife, a little girl, and of course Dr. Lewis. It was a small intimate group with one aim—to be a blessing to the people of Dominican Republic. Our collective goal was to give of ourselves totally to the people and the cause during our short stay. As a group, we were asked to bring clothing down for the children, gently used clothes to donate to children and mothers in the communities there.

We ended up collecting more than 500 pounds of clothing and we brought it all over in extra suitcases that we checked in on our flights. When we arrived, we knew that we were somewhere very different. It was somewhat of a tropical paradise. Palm trees, tropical fruit trees, lizards and iguanas were all a part of the welcoming scenery, along with the beautiful ocean. When we arrived at our hotel, the RIU Grand, I was a bit confused at first. The hotel was amazing with all of the amenities that one could ask for, breakfast, lunch, and full buffet dinner.

It was a 4 ½ star resort with several pools, restaurants, bars, and a host of entertainment options. I was confused because when I typically thought about missions, my mind immediately shifted to the worst living conditions, no running water, limited electricity, abject poverty, starving children and so on. Even John the businessman who traveled with us thought that we'd be staying in depressing surroundings for the week. In fact, John had been on a previous trip to Dominican with another mission group a few years earlier. He told us how the experience was quite different.

This church group went there to physically build a church and school with bricks and mortar. John, who is in his seventies, was all-in and ready to help. They stayed in meager barracks, no buffet, no swimming pools, no beach water, and certainly no entertainment. He just remembers working hard, lifting bricks, and having to see the doctor for severe back pain when he returned back home to Connecticut because he lifted heavy bricks that threw out his back. Although he helped build a structure on that trip, his most dominant memory was badly hurting his back.

Giving Back Doesn't Mean Taking Away

John asked Dr. Lewis why he provided top-notch accommodations for the people traveling with him. John thought that the worse the conditions, the more we'd feel like we were giving back. Dr. Lewis, laughed at his question for a moment and then jokingly said to John, John this trip isn't about back breaking; it's about giving of yourself. We want you to go back home empty, because you gave everything you could, yet full of joy in knowing that you pleased God in doing so.

Dr. Lewis, who had been on mission trips in the jungle and who had lived in shacks and shanties knew all sides of the mission field, having traveled for 30 years to countries in South America, Europe, Asia and even Native American reservations. Lewis' philosophy was that if at all possible, the volunteer workers should live in the finest accommodations possible during their stay. The better the accommodations, the better the group will feel. They will be refreshed, having eaten good food, relaxed and ready to do the work needed for long hours without excuse.

If they weren't in the best environment, they would have the limitations associated with being tired, hot, and hungry. Dr. Lewis wanted no excuses, so he made sure that we had the best accommodations, taking all excuses away not to serve. The first day we just settled in, unpacked our clothing, made dinner reservations and simply relaxed after a very long travel day. The next morning, we had an amazing cook-to-order breakfast accompanied with fresh fruit drinks and a complete buffet as well. We relaxed on the resort and was told to be ready for the start of our missions in the early afternoon.

Early afternoon, the Pastor who was hosting us, Pastor Eliezer Diaz Mejia, came to pick us up. He came in a white van that only seated about 8 folks. He asked one of his parishioners to drive along with their car to carry extra persons. Leaving the hotel was the beginning of our amazing mission trip as we headed out from Punta Cana to Higuey, nearly a 50-minute rocky road ride. On our way, we began to see the beautiful people that we were called to help. I brought my portable adjustment table on the trip.

My desire was to make sure that I was ready to serve as many people as my body could handle. We went to the church, and Dr. Lewis was speaking in English, while Pastor Eliezer translated every word into Spanish. Pastor "Eli" as he is affectionately referred to is a gentle and loving man who is arguably one of the most spirited translators I've ever seen. This man truly has passion for what he does and there is no doubt that he is called to be a preacher and pastor. When you watch him, you realize that he is in his zone.

Dr. Lewis, an amazingly gifted orator, preached a message about destiny and hope. The people were sitting on the edges of their seats eagerly awaiting to be inspired through each word that he spoke. After the service, the people stayed behind as they were instructed to. Pastor Eli told them that there was a health couple from the United States that would give them adjustments to relieve their pain. At that time, Pastor Eli introduced me and Dr. Dawn and began translating for us. I began to teach them for about 20 minutes or so, exactly what chiropractic was and how it could help them.

The people were amazed by what I taught them, yet they really didn't have a concept of what it meant to be adjusted; what vertebral subluxation was, or how chiropractor can help to reduce pain in their body. At that point, I knew that I would have to begin demonstrating for the people how chiropractic works. We lined up nearly 20 people in the front of the church where we set up our make-shift clinic. Nearly 100 other people were waiting for their adjustments. I began by first adjustment Pastor Eli and Dr. Lewis. I felt that they should be the ice-breakers.

While I was adjusting them, you could hear the reactions of the people in the audience, oohs and aahs. No one in the entire church had ever heard of a chiropractor in their lives. We came introducing a totally new concept to them, one that would change their lives forever. I adjusted many people after the service. I spent nearly 3 hours checking and adjusting people for subluxation. There were people who were nearly paralyzed from accidents, trauma, and other life altering moments. Some of the people could hardly move.

Others confessed that they lived with the pain because they didn't believe that there was a possibility of ever

> I realized that giving back didn't take anything away from me. Giving of myself was only increasing me more.

being healed. I remember some of the people crying and sobbing, not because they were sad, but because they were filled with so much joy in knowing that they no longer had to suffer. Some came in limping and they left walking straight and upright. People who had suffered with neck and back pain for a decade suddenly were pain free. It was surreal. The people were receptive.

It was in that moment that I realized that I was giving of myself in a way that brought healing to me. I was dealing with my own problems with my infected bone in my toe that hadn't properly healed since the spider bite. That often pained me. My balance had sometimes been off, and I could only do short stints of adjusting as it would tire me out rather quickly. However, in this moment all of that went away. It was as if I was being healed as I was helping to heal these people. I realized that giving back didn't take anything away from me. Giving of myself was only increasing me more.

This is a message not only for chiropractors, but everyone. Life is a mission. And you and everyone else are on the mission field in some way or another. Maybe it's not in the Dominican Republic or in Soweto township near Johannesburg South Africa. Maybe it's not in Lima Peru or San Paulo Brazil, Beijing, China, or Romania. Wherever you are you can be intentional to give of yourself in a meaningful way. My point is that there is no excuse for not giving back. It can be in the city of Syracuse, Bronx, Hartford, Detroit, Los Angeles or Chicago.

> There is no excuse for not giving back.

Wherever you are there are people who need your help, your love, your expertise, your hands. When you lend your hands to others you create in that selfsame moment an energy field of love and purpose. While I was adjusting the patients, Dr. Dawn ministered to dozens of people simultaneously. Dr. Dawn works in the very rare field of Energy Medicine and energy healing. There are few people in the world with her training. Combined with prayer, Dr. Dawn began to work with people who had negative baggage in their lives that they've carried around for decades.

Dr. Dawn worked with several people one-on-one to help them rid themselves of that negative garbage that has been holding them back far too long. The people were in complete amazement by the miracles that were happening. They had no idea that a few folks from the United States were coming to help improve their lives and cope with problems in life that otherwise seemed impossible. It was one of the greatest weeks of my and Dr. Dawn's life. We were all there as a labor of love to bless an entire nation. We all left our jobs behind for the week to give more than we'd ever expected back in return.

> When you lend your hands to others you create in that selfsame moment an energy field of love and purpose.

> To learn to be thankful with limited clothing, limited food, limited recreation, is quite remarkable, especially for those whose lives are driven by material gain.

One of the highlights for the week is when we visited an orphanage for little toddler boys. We went there to give them clothing, candy, and chiropractic care. They were so delighted that we came to visit them, as they don't have many foreign visitors come through. When we left some of the little ones began to tear up as they thought they'd never see us again. We all promised that we'd come back and visit them again, a promise that I will surely keep. Just watching the orphans, and how ecstatic and grateful they were just because of our visit, made me realize how much more thankful I should be for the daily blessings that God gives me.

To learn to be thankful with limited clothing, limited food, limited recreation, is quite remarkable, especially for those whose lives are driven by material gain. Why do I mention these events and details from our mission to Dominican Republic? I want you to realize and recognize that a great part of your life and your vitality is connected to serving. You will live a more fruitful and productive life when you consider others in need. And remember, there are always people in need. Chiropractors can adjust homeless people or people who cannot afford their services.

Accountants can offer free tax services to people who earn low annual incomes. Many lawyers give pro bono services to clients who cannot afford their services. Surgeons do medical missions to help correct cleft palate, and other deformities in children. Young people: you can mow the elderly neighbor's lawn or take their garbage out on garbage day. Go grocery shopping for an elderly

> Chiropractors can adjust homeless people or people who cannot afford their services.

person. This list can go on and on forever. The point is that if you are unable to board a plane to the Dominican Republic you can create a mission field wherever you are. And when you do that you are not only helping the people you are giving services to, you are helping yourself.

Ways to Give Back

Don't limit yourself or limit your blessing. There are so many ways to give back. If you want to create a life of giving back there are many organizations that could use your monetary donations, your volunteering, clothing donations, advice, and many other volunteer services. There are extremely large non-profits such as United Way, YMCA, YWCA, Boy Scouts, Girl Scouts, Boys and Girls Clubs of America, Feed the Poor, American Society for the Prevention of Cruelty to Animals, American Red Cross,

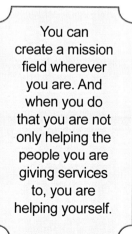

> You can create a mission field wherever you are. And when you do that you are not only helping the people you are giving services to, you are helping yourself.

> Don't limit yourself or limit your blessing. There are so many ways to give back.

and Habitat for Humanity. These organizations have a track record of providing services to people and animals. These organizations are always in need of a helping hand. If you google any them you will find out more information about what they do and how you can get involved.

Dr. Lewis sponsors a mission trip at least once a year to Dominican Republic. He is always in need of chiropractors who are willing to give up 5 to 7 days of their lives to touch people hearts. He is also looking for other volunteer professions, dentists, physicians, carpenters, brick layers, electricians, plumbers and veterinarians. This is just a short list of people who can help. He needs people in nearly every field. You can email Dr. Lewis directly to find out more information about the mission trips, upcoming dates and how you can get involved at draaron@thescribesink.com.

Dr. Lewis is also the founder of The Scribe's Institute, Inc which is a literacy and S.T.E.M. based organization in Hartford, CT that teaches children in grades 2nd to 8th how to become the best readers, writers, scientists, and technological minds in the world. His organization always welcomes donations, professionals to speak on their profession, food donations, and other volunteers. You can find out more at www.thescribesinstitute.com .

> It doesn't matter whether you are 9 years old or 90 years young, you can give back. You can do it!

Whatever you choose to do, as NIKE said, "Just Do It." We wholeheartedly believe that when you begin to invest your life into missions, not only will your healing happen, but you will be blessed with everything you need to continue going forward. This book is all about getting your life back. It's about knowing that it's never too late to improve your health and your overall life. You'll know that you have new life when you are able to share it with others. It doesn't matter whether you are 9 years old or 90 years young, you can give back. You can do it!

Chapter Seven

TAKE BACK YOUR LIFE

A couple of years ago, a colleague of mine had to go to have some blood work done. This is his story.

"I typically go and get bloodwork done annually just to make sure that everything in my body is functioning well. For physicals and bloodwork, I typically go to a medical doctor since my insurance pays for it and since it's routine practice for most doctors to conduct physicals and order bloodwork for testing. As I was sitting down, I can remember the physician telling me what drugs I should be taking. I mean, she was telling me about drugs I need to take as if it were standard practice, like taking a bath or eating breakfast.

She didn't know I was a chiropractor. And neither did she know that I didn't take drugs at all. She tested me, told me that my blood pressure was high, my glucose was high, and my cholesterol was high. Since this is MY LIFE that she was commenting about, I felt that the responsible thing to do was to ask to see my own lab results. Most people never ask for lab results, they typically just take what the doctor says as truth. That is a very dangerous thing to do. This is your life, you should always ask questions. And if a doctor gets sheepish or tries to avoid answering your questions, that should raise a major red flag.

Well a red flag was raised for me. She asked me, "Why do you need to see the lab results?" I told her simply that I wanted to see them for myself. Fasting, my glucose was 100mg/dL. Perhaps that was high for this laboratory's averages. Hgb A1C was 4.1% (WLN according to this lab), total cholesterol was 156 mg/dL, HDL was 59 mg/dL and LDL was 130 mg/dl (borderline high for this laboratory's averages. My blood pressure was 124/68. I certainly didn't see how that was an issue at all as she proceeded to tell me that I was borderline hypertensive and diabetic and that I should immediately start taking blood pressure medication, stains, and metformin.

"And you should know the truth and the truth shall make you free."

Needless to say, I refused her offer, and told her that I thought that she was completely nuts. I asked her how could she make a lifelong decision based on one reading, a reading that could very well have been skewed? When I asked her that she had no answer to give me, yet still trying to persuade me to take the medication. Having no success in convincing me to take the medication she inquisitively enquired what I did for a living. Proudly, I told her that I was a chiropractor. She brusquely responded, "That figures."

At that point, we exchanged a few choice words. Then she started to sneeze. She sneezed again. As I grabbed my paperwork and hurried out of the room, I told her that it would probably be a good idea to begin taking Zyrtec for her allergies. She told me that there was no need because she didn't have allergies. I told her, "My point exactly." There wasn't any need in her taking allergy medication based on two sneezes. That would be ridiculous. But it was just as ridiculous for her to suggest that I need to be on hypertension, diabetic, and high cholesterol medication based on one laboratory test."

"And you should know the truth and the truth shall make you free." I'm not bound by drugs because I was raised drug free, raised knowing the truth. More than that, my parents instilled in me that my life was my life and that I was responsible for protecting it at all cost. There are so many people who have freely given over their lives to a culture of drugs because they do not realize that they have a choice in the matter.

In the story that I just shared about my colleague, so many average people, probably 90% or more would have just accepted the doctor's mere suggestion and began taking a series of harmful drugs that they didn't even need. Most people don't ask questions, and the few that may ask questions tend to ask the wrong ones. When he asked the doctor about the validity of the lab tests and why he should take these drugs, she could not give him a straight answer. Instead she danced around the question and just insisted on him taking drugs that would have had no benefit to him at all.

The truth is, his story is not really all that unique. Everyday people are given suggestions and orders that they don't have to comply with, yet they think they have to because of the status quo. Imagine if people like Rev. Dr. Martin Luther King Jr. never challenged racial injustice and inequality in the United States and just accepted injustice as the way things should be where would we be as a society? Where would we be if woman never fought for their rights to fair and equal pay to men working the same jobs? These questions can go on and on.

> Imagine if people like Rev. Dr. Martin Luther King Jr. never challenged racial injustice and inequality in the United States and just accepted injustice as the way things should be where would we be as a society?

The point is that this is your life and you have every right to know what goes into your body. You have every right to say no. Say no to drugs. Say not to that which you do not believe will help you. Say no to anything that can potentially harm you. And ask questions, lots of them. Remember, this movie is called "Your Life." You are the writer, the producer, and the director. More than that, you are the star. You have to preserve yourself, because the earth needs you. We all need you. I've listed some practical ways that you can start right now with getting your life back. There's no better time than the present to begin this course.

1. Make time for yourself because you are the most important person on earth.

You are priority number one. Far too often, people who give the most of themselves to help others find themselves at a deficit. They aren't at a shortfall for giving, they're at a shortfall because they haven't recognized the need to give back to themselves. Why are you the most important person on earth? The answer is rather easy.

You have to preserve yourself, because the earth needs you. We all need you.

Without you, nothing that you are called to do will ever get done. No one can do what you do, quite like you. So, it is necessary to preserve you to get the job done that you were designed to fulfill. In order to do that you will need to understand the value of me-time, time for yourself.

I'd like to ask you a question. What do you want to do, now? No, I didn't ask you what you were going to do or with whom you were going to do it. I want to know: what do want to do? There are so many people who cannot answer that question because their lives are so caught up in trying to please others, so much so, that they've totally lost themselves. In getting your life back, you have to make yourself a priority while serving others. Most days in the week I adjust patients. I block off dedicated time to make sure that I can serve as many people as possible.

> Without you, nothing that you are called to do will ever get done.

However, when it is "me time," I make sure to do things that I enjoy. I enjoy travel, especially to beautiful Caribbean islands such as the Cayman Islands. As much as I can, I like to get away and just relax, regroup and refresh myself. Without that time away, that "me time," I could have never lasted as long as I have. That time helped me to heal physical, spiritually, and emotionally. As I grew older, I also grew wiser and began to understand how to block off time for me. That time is the best time, as I regroup so that I can relaunch.

Dr. Lewis has an insane schedule. He wears many hats. As a professional writer, he's up at 5 A.M. while its quiet before the day starts and he is writing five days a week, a minimum of 4000 words a day. He's always working on books, blogs, letters and social media so he has to be sure to stay ahead of the curve. He publishes dozens of books each year through his publishing company. Lewis also runs a non-profit organization, The Scribe's Institute that serves the educational needs of children in his city in elementary and middle school. Lewis runs four 5-week Cohorts each year serving more than 100 children.

On Sundays, and Wednesdays he delivers the message to his congregation. He counsels parishioners, visits and prays for the sick and shut in, and visits the prisons. Also, he operates a home remodeling company and restores old homes. He travels around the world teaching and addressing the needs of people in developing nations, with regards to improving child education and how to improve healthcare. He's an active father of 5 adult children and an overactive 3-year-old granddaughter.

In a peak year he travels about 150,000 miles in the air. He's established and supports missions in 4 countries, in South America, Central America, the Caribbean, and Africa. Oh, I forgot to mention, that he's running for mayor of the city of Hartford as well. How can he possibly find time for himself with such an overloaded schedule? Dr. Lewis is a jazz aficionado. As much as he can, he gets away to listen to live jazz in Hartford, New Haven, Old Lyme, Boston, and New York.

Every morning he rides his bike for about 10-15 miles before going into the office. Every 5 years or so he trains for a 26-mile marathon. At least once a week he eats Vietnamese food, his favorite. Without taking the me-time, he would have burnt out a long time ago. It's not too late to create the life that you desire. However, you have to take the initiative to do what you believe best serves you. You have to create what I call that "sacred space" that helps you to replenish and energizes you to do more, give more, and enjoy more.

2. Stop trying to fit so you can stand out

> You weren't called to fit in, you were called to stand out.

Let's face it. Being different and thinking different isn't a sport for the weak. Our entire culture supports you most when you do what everybody else does, think like everybody else thinks, and live in the status quo of life. While that may be safe, there really isn't any growth and development in living that way. God made each and every person uniquely distinctive. There are no two people who are exactly the same. Even people who are born twins, grow to discover that they have just as many things that are different than the same about them.

You weren't called to fit in, you were called to stand out. Chiropractors in general are not people who were called to fit in a certain mold. We are different. We regularly challenge big giants like the pharmaceutical industry and we do it fearlessly. We take on the promoters of vaccinations and expose their lies. It's clear that we don't fit in, and we don't want to. At least the chiropractors that I hang out with, don't want to fit in. There is always a price to pay for being different, holding on to your convictions, and living your life out loud, even if it doesn't fit the conventional standards of society. The only other option is mediocrity.

3. Learn how to say no.

"No" can often be a far more powerful word than "yes." Have you ever heard of a yes person? A yes person always agrees with everyone, everywhere, all the time because they are just a bit fearful about the repercussions they might receive if they say no. They go along to get along. It's interesting, that adult peer pressure can be just as destructive as teen peer pressure. When teenagers yield to the whims of their friends, and succumb to drugs such as opioids and cocaine, we often wonder why they wouldn't be stronger; why won't they just say no? While it may be wrong for them, consider yourself as well.

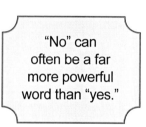

"No" can often be a far more powerful word than "yes."

To what do you continue to say "yes" to, when you should be saying "no"? Like a pressured teenager, are you saying yes to fit in, to be accepted? If so, then check yourself. A famous real estate investor Dolf DeRoos, once said that you make most of your money in real esate on the deals you say no to. Imagine that if you start saying no to more things, maybe it'll free up your time to complete the things you've said yes to. It's a natural feeling to want to please everyone in life, but honestly, you can't. After living many years I'm not sure if there's a secret to success in life.

It's a natural feeling to want to please everyone in life, but honestly, you can't.

Personally, I believe that success is defined differently for each person.

> The secret to failure is in trying to please everybody.

How we have measured success may not be the best formula to use as a measure. However, I have discovered the secret to failure. The secret to failure is in trying to please everybody. When you say no to things that you either cannot do, or shouldn't do, or really don't want to do, you add life to your life. It's all about being principled. Living a principled life often starts with saying no, even to good things.

4. Do something different for a change.

Boredom has become bliss for so many people. People get up each day at the same time, go to the same job, work with the same people, and then get off at the same time. They go home, and eat the same meal, in the same kitchen, cooked on the same stove. They wash the same dishes in the same sink, watch the same show on Netflix for the same amount of time. They eat the same snack, go off to bed at the same time, on the same mattress and pillow. Then they wake up the next day and do it again. That's not life!

> It's not worth traveling all the way through life only to discover at the end that you've never lived life at all.

Imagine what life would be like if, every now and again, you just switched things up. Skip your routine breakfast and buy breakfast instead. Don't always eat the lunch you brought with you to work. Go out and have lunch with your co-workers. No Netflix tonight, go to the movies

124

instead, watch it in 3-D. Forget about your I-Pod today and find somewhere to listen to live music. The point is that your life becomes more fruitful and exciting when you choose to do something different for a change. Yes, there are some things that are predictable in life, but it doesn't always have to be you.

Make a commitment to do something so out of the ordinary, that people begin to ask questions. Go jump out of a plane. Go bungy jumping. Hike a mountain, run a marathon, eat octopus. If it's different, try it for the sake of expansion. Expand your mind. Travel somewhere you've never been before. The idea is to get out of your comfort zone so that you can not only enjoy life but experience it in the process. It's not worth traveling all the way through life only to discover at the end that you've never lived life at all.

5. Trust the process and learn from it.

Trusting the process may be the hardest task of all. On some level most of us are controllers. We want to always know how things will turn out. We want to have security and feel safe and supported all of the time. None of those things are bad at all. The problem is, that isn't how life works. There are times when you will give all that you have and receive nothing in return from the ones you gave to. You

> We must be committed to learn the lesson that life is trying to teach. Life is always teaching us a lesson, unfortunately we rarely show up to class on time.

may lose your investment. Your children may not always get along with you or see eye to eye with you. You may find yourself getting divorced. You may lose your job. You may have to file for bankruptcy.

Listen, this is not a list a downers and negatives just for the sake of being negative. I'm not a negative person at all. However, I have lived life and I am fully aware that things do happen. When things happen, we must be committed to learn the lesson that life is trying to teach. Life is always teaching us a lesson, unfortunately we rarely show up to class on time. I don't wish any of those negative things on you. What I want you to take away is that even if those things do happen to you, you'll stay committed to the course that you've been set on.

You won't give up because life threw a curve ball. When things happen, they do so because life is trying to get you to discover what you are really made of. What is your real worth and value? You can never know what the value of a diamond is until it has gone through a process. Before a diamond is refined it looks very much like a lump of coal. There's nothing that's attractive about it at all. But after that diamond goes through a process, it's value increases dramatically. It's the same thing with you and your life.

If you've never gone through anything in life, not only would you have not learned anything, your value would be low, and would decrease rapidly. The things you go through in life, once you've conquered them, makes you stronger and wiser. Don't avoid the process because it'll show up somewhere else at another time. If you don't pass the test the first go round, you'll have to take it again. Go through your process and learn from it. Yes, you are that diamond in the rough. And after you've gone through the process you will shine.

Just remember that you are not the only one who is going through a process in life. I've been through a process, we've all been through various processes. You are not alone. You will live the life that was originally designed for you to live. Whatever you may be dealing with right now, it won't last. This too shall pass. And when you come out, I promise, I'll be waiting for you. So, let's get started, because It's Not Too Late.

About Authors

Dr. Timothy Schaub has been a chiropractor for 40 years. Dr. Schaub has been an adjunct professor at NY Chiropractic College and he has earned membership into the Chiropractic Knights of the Roundtable. He was awarded Chiropractor of the Year by Parker Chiropractic Research Foundation and is the founder of ChiroSushi Summit. Dr. Schaub operates a successful practice in Homer, New York.

Dr. Aaron Lewis is a human rights activist, best-selling author, publisher, spiritual leader, educator, and chiropractic ambassador. He has written for his clients more than 160 books and has traveled to more that 60 countries helping to reform and shape the future of healthcare and education. He lives in New England.